—150—
RESTAURANTS
YOU NEED
TO VISIT BEFORE
—YOU DIE—

By Amélie Vincent,
The Foodalist.

LANNOO

OVERVIEW

OVERVIEW

OVERVIEW

🌍

AFRICA

🌍

ASIA

OVERVIEW

Introduction

By Amélie Vincent *The Foodalist*

I have always been attracted to human beings, as I believe in the magical power to instill a bit of love and joy into the hearts of others. As a child, I wanted to be a nurse or a social worker, with the primary aim to help others to have a better life. I ended up as becoming a lawyer after eight years of training in four different, major cities... Yet, something was still missing.

I decided to entirely change my course – through difficult, life-changing moments. I launched The Foodalist (@thefoodalist, www.thefoodalist.com), a content agency specialized in international gastronomy and chefs.

Food had indeed always been an important part of my life, as I was raised by curious parents from multicultural backgrounds who frenetically explored the world through cultural aspects, including food. Growing up as an only child, I used to be the tiny invader in kitchens, experiencing a wide range of colors, smells, and flavors, before falling asleep on the knees of my beloved mother, using a tablecloth as a pillow.

Through all my projects, words and images for more than seven years, my intention has been to pay homage to the people who inspired me through my life's roughest moments with their sense of bravura, dedication and passion, namely the chefs. I see them as important figures, holding an essential role model in a world that has become more globalized, but also more commercial and superficial. First, chefs are humans with noble minds, working extremely hard to provide pleasure to others, from what they find in Mother nature.

Those rare personalities do understand and transmit values that are way more important than money and image. For thousands of years, they have been bonding us as a human community, around tables, sharing culture and identity through the most universal and powerful way humans have ever experienced: food.

In this world in need of hopes and values, I see chefs as generous hearts and artists who can give inspiration today, to build a better world tomorrow. As Vassily Kandinsky once said: "Art in general is not a creation without purpose. It is a power whose aim must be to develop and improve the human soul." Yes, I do believe gastronomy is an art, and food has that power.

Why *150 Restaurants You Need to Visit before You Die*?

Of course, each selection is subjective and each choice hard to make. The international scene is ever evolving, and what is there today may no longer be there tomorrow.

This book is created as a visual bucket list of memorable worldwide experiences, compiling both food and atmosphere through my eyes, in order for curious gourmets to find visual and informative samples of the current food scene. And, of course there are much more than 150 restaurants worth a visit, and way more human beings to discover inside their kitchen, in any part of the world, and even at the corner of our street ...

— 01 —
TASTING COUNTER

| UNITED STATES | Boston 14 Tyler Street, Somerville, MA 02143 | CHEF'S COUNTER |

◆ TO VISIT BEFORE YOU DIE BECAUSE

It's an innovative experience to have dinner in the Aeronaut Brewing company space.

Tasting Counter is chef Peter Ungár's innovative concept in which he has created a dining experience that focuses on the guests to provide them a memorable dining event. First, diners purchase tickets for lunch or dinner online beforehand, so they do not need to bring any money to the restaurant. Then, inspired by the omakase style, from the Japanese phrase meaning 'I'll leave it to you' (the chef), the guests create an online profile that will help the chef get to know them and their palate, and they choose a drinks pairing option (wine, beer, sake or non-alcoholic beverages). Finally, in the small space that seats up to 20, the culinary theatre plunges the guests into a multisensory dining experience, watching the team performing the choreographed acts of prepping, plating and serving each course in front of them. The menu might feature an island of lobster custard and seaweed in a briny pool of uni (sea urchin) broth, tangy sour-cream dumplings with crispy pancetta, and bite-size chocolate ganache cake with preserved strawberries. Operating under the '0 carbon, 50 local, 100 natural' philosophy, Tasting Counter strives towards a zero-carbon footprint, sourcing a minimum of 50 per cent of its products from within Massachusetts.

tastingcounter.com

— 02 —
AMANGIRI

UNITED
STATES

Canyon Point
1 Kayenta Road, Canyon Point, UT 84741

MODERN
AMERICAN

◆ TO VISIT BEFORE YOU DIE BECAUSE

The view of the rock formations and the arid desert is spectacular.

Sitting about a mile from the Arizona border in Canyon Point, surrounded by breathtaking rock formations and the arid desert, the Amangiri, or 'peaceful mountain', incorporates the amazing landscape into its design by using muted browns. Within this natural interior, the cuisine is inspired by the American Southwest and is made primarily from locally sourced ingredients carefully selected by the chef. Meals are served from the open kitchen to tables that look out through floor-to-ceiling windows over the changing colours of the Utah desert, next to the sublime outdoor dining terrace and the peaceful pool.

— 03 —
BELLEMORE

UNITED STATES	Chicago 564 W. Randolph Street, Chicago, IL 60661	MODERN AMERICAN

◆ TO VISIT BEFORE YOU DIE BECAUSE

It is a wonderful experience to arrive early for a drink in the plush lounge and taste the innovative cocktails such as the horchata-like Pumpkin Seed Milk.

Every inch of the Bellemore bears the opulence of an old French manor house. Among the brass chandeliers, wood columns, vintage mirrors and stuffed birds perched above the marble bar, chef Jimmy Papadopoulos's menu is a fitting kind of feast for this prestigious decor: seasonal American fare with luxurious touches. A sliver of oyster-custard pie is topped with Osetra caviar and dill-speckled crème fraîche while crunchy pumpkin seeds and whipped gorgonzola-filled cannoli electrify an autumn salad of port-braised quince and grilled beetroots. The chef changes the menu according to which ingredients are in season, and the cocktail list is managed by Boka Group beverage director Lee Zaremba, using house-made tonics and other inventive components.

www.bellemorechicago.com

— 04 —
SMYTH

Chicago
177 North Ada Street, Chicago, IL 60607

MODERN
AMERICAN

◆ TO VISIT BEFORE YOU DIE BECAUSE

Here there is the opportunity to taste combinations that are both familiar and unexpected, such as raw oysters served with apple granita or Dungeness crab and crab brains topped with cooked foie gras, in a casual setting.

In Chicago's West Loop neighbourhood, husband-and-wife team John Shields (formerly sous chef at Grant Achatz's Alinea restaurant) and Karen Urie Shields brought their pedigreed experience to Smyth, a spacious and modern restaurant with open-air kitchens, contemporary furnishings and large windows. Earning two Michelin stars in less than two years, they have created some genuine magic with seasonally driven multi-course menus thanks to a strong relationship with a 20-acre farm just outside of Chicago.

The chefs' connection with the soil yields such items as beetroot bolognese, scallops and Jerusalem artichokes cloaked in brown butter, and smoked oxtail tacos with hay and Marmite. Downstairs The Loyalist, a bar with concrete floors, dark walls and amber-hued lighting, serves more casual food, including burgers, oysters and aged rib-eye grilled with brown butter. The two places offer two completely different experiences, but both are executed with aplomb.

— 05 —
LA GUARIDA

Havana

CUBA

Concordia 418 / Gervasio y Escobar,
Centro Habana, Ciudad de la Habana Cuba

INTERNATIONAL

◆ TO VISIT BEFORE YOU DIE BECAUSE

**It is wonderful to immerse yourself in a bygone time,
in this charming paladar that evokes the Old Cuba.**

With its headless statue, the entrance of La Mansión Camagüey welcomes you like a scene from a 1940s film noir, and its splendour pervades from its magnificent wooden entrance door to the marble staircase that leads up to the most legendary private restaurant in the city. Inside, the place itself evokes an ageing Parisian café, with its a warm atmosphere, soft lights, fine table linen and silver cutlery. The food includes the best Havana products and dishes, such as rabbit pâté, oxtail risotto and grouper fish in a white wine, orange or sweet-and-sour sauce.

— 06 —
ASTRID Y GASTÓN

Lima
Av. Paz Soldán 290, San Isidro, Lima

MODERN
PERUVIAN

◆ TO VISIT BEFORE YOU DIE BECAUSE

Chef Gastón Acurio's signature dish is the 'cebiche of love', a tasty creation referencing the many migrants to Peru, who have integrated with each other and celebrate diversity in peace.

Gastón Acurio is the architect of the Peruvian culinary movement. He began his studies in law school, and changed to working with food when he entered Le Cordon Bleu, Paris. While abroad he met his German-born wife Astrid, who was also working towards a career in the kitchen. The couple returned to Peru and founded their eponymous restaurant, Astrid y Gastón. Originally with a French theme, Acurio decided to slowly make some changes and to focus exclusively on Peruvian culture, dishes and ingredients. The pioneering restaurant is responsible for helping transform Peruvian cuisine to what it is today. The restaurant is located in a 300-year-old former plantation house named 'Moreyra House', and hosts a fine-dining restaurant, a gastrobar, a botanical garden, two private rooms with their own kitchens and bars, and a research and development lab. Acurio's signature dish, the 'cebiche of love', combines sea urchin, scallops, river shrimp, lime, red onions, corn, sweet potatoes, plantains and coriander, referencing the many migrants in Peru, who have integrated with each other in peace.

PERU	Lima	MODERN
	Av. Pedro de Osma 301, Barranco, Lima	PERUVIAN

◆ TO VISIT BEFORE YOU DIE BECAUSE

The bar is based on an exploration of the country's biodiversity; the tasting menus transport diners to different altitudes. To enhance the experience, try the house-made 'High Jungle cocoa cacao' cocktail.

Chef Virgilio Martínez with his wife Pía León has achieved much for his country's gastronomy in recent years, helping to promote Peruvian cuisine around the world. He also works with his sister Malena's research project, Mater Iniciativa, to help discover and educate on local agriculture and ingredients in the Andes and Amazon region. In the new location, customers pass through the garden filled with native coastal plants, a fire lit inside a traditional Peruvian huatia oven and a solar dehydrator. Inside, the restaurant features an open kitchen with an entrance surrounded by glass and Amazonian wood walls and a dining space filled with grey stone tables. Based on an exploration of the country's biodiversity, tasting menus transport diners to different altitudes and ecosystems through each course, featuring unusual Amazonian fishes, strange fruits, unique jungle plants and curious mountain herbs. Expect a colourful journey through numerous wonderful ingredients you have never heard of, such as dragon's blood tree resin and cassava starch, or red Amazon pacha fish with airampo, a cactus of the region.

— 08 —
MAIDO

PERU

Lima
399 San Martin Street (at the corner with Colon Street), Miraflores, Lima

NIKKEI

◆ TO VISIT BEFORE YOU DIE BECAUSE

The 'choripan', a chorizo sausage made from an innovative mix of fish and octopus, is served in a bun in a hotdog box.

In the Miraflores district in Lima, in a hip urban space with a laid-back vibe, the Japanese Peruvian-born chef Mitsuharu Tsumura provides his interpretation of Nikkei cuisine, which is a blend of the local tastes with the intricate flavours and techniques brought to Peru by Japanese migrants. On the wooden tables of the minimalist Japanese-style decor, Maido's tasting menu is presented on ceramics, draped on rocks or served in Martini glasses, with highlights including a fusion sushi topped with duck and foie gras, a confit guinea pig with Japanese noodles or a ceviche in a seashell on a bed of yellow peppers frozen with liquid nitrogen. Chef Mitsuharu Tsumura wants diners to have physical contact with the food, which is why many dishes are served without cutlery.

UNITED STATES	Los Angeles	MODERN AMERICAN
	3599 Hayden Avenue, Culver City, CA 90232	

◆ TO VISIT BEFORE YOU DIE BECAUSE

Here you can explore one of the newest immersive culinary experiences the whole food planet is talking about.

In Los Angeles, in an area of low-key white buildings, Vespertine is an immersive restaurant that looks like a futuristic building dedicated to 'exploring a dimension of cuisine that is neither rooted in tradition nor culture'. With waiters wearing avant-garde black uniforms, and a 3D printer that produces moulds for sculpting ingredients in the kitchen, the young chef Jordan Kahn – who previously worked at Per Se and Alinea – aims to create an everlasting memory for the guests, believing that atmosphere is as crucial as the food itself. The music, for example, is one of the most important parts of the whole experience. The first soundtrack plays as you enter on the ground floor and as you approach the lift. Another track will start on the second floor, when the chef welcomes you by name, while a different sound plays on the roof, where you sit in futuristic lounge chairs and enjoy half a dozen amuse-bouches and snacks, overlooking Culver City and the mountains. Finally, there is music in the 22-seat dining room, where spaceship food is served to the customers who sit on a steel-and-wool banquette.

— 10 —
WILLOWS INN

UNITED
STATES

Lummi Island
2579 West Shore Drive, Lummi Island, WA 98262

MODERN
AMERICAN

◆ TO VISIT BEFORE YOU DIE BECAUSE

To complete the immersive gourmet experience, you can spend a night in the beachside guest houses by the sea.

Willows Inn on Lummi Island is a calm and peaceful location far away from the hustle and bustle of everyday life and is also a truly sustainable work of art. It takes three hours from Seattle to reach the remote island, where Willows Inn sits perched above a beautiful pebble beach. This is the fabulous place where Blaine Wetzel, one of the hottest and most talented young chefs in the USA, serves the meticulously local cuisine, thanks to the approach he developed during his three years as chef de partie at Noma. Inspired by quality and simplicity,

Wetzel is primarily forage-focused, using the ingredients he finds in the local forests or in the sea nearby. Throughout the evening's 22-course meal, the staff introduces each dish and its origins, and prepares the freshest ingredients such as salmon smoked in the restaurant's own smokehouse, oysters from the surrounding waters and wild grains and fruits gathered from the fields. The restaurant hibernates for the winter season, giving time for Wetzel and his team to explore new places and cuisines for the coming year.

www.willows-inn.com

— 11 —
MIL

PERU

Maras
Vía a Moray, Maras

MODERN
PERUVIAN

◆ TO VISIT BEFORE YOU DIE BECAUSE

This is a worldwide talked-about dining experience, which also has a laboratory that overlooks the stunning Peruvian landscape.

At restaurant Mil in the Andes, chef Virgilio Martìnez from Central in Lima has created Latin America's most talked-about dining experience, that is, a restaurant and a laboratory that focuses on Peruvian culture, produce and identity. Set 3,500 metres above sea level, Mil is located in the Sacred Valley, a 45-minute drive from Cusco, on the edge of the ruins at Moray. Housed within a former vicuña breeding centre, Martìnez together with his team and his anthropologist Francesco d'Angelo want guests to touch the Andean earth first, understand the work of its local communities and then to eat from it. Which is why diners access the entrance to the restaurant by walking along one side of the rustic building and through a passage with herbs strung across three lines. In the research centre focused on the local diversity, the team of anthropologists, scientists and farmers are focusing their studies on coffee, cacao and root vegetables to understand its nutrients and production hand in hand with the local communities. Mil's eight-step menu, paired with infusions prepared in-house such as sun-dried cacao nib tea, showcases strictly regional ingredients, with light dishes focusing on vegetables, tubers and grains, and a little protein coming mainly from alpaca and llama: tunta, which is freeze-dried potato for dipping in tamarillo uchucuta salsa, and lamb tartare topped with pink petals teamed with a crunchy white quinoa salad, plated on beautiful dishware handcrafted from local wood and stone.

— 12 —
PUJOL

	Mexico City	
MEXICO	Tennyson 133, Polanco V Sección, CP 11560, CDMX	MODERN MEXICAN

◆ TO VISIT BEFORE YOU DIE BECAUSE

Pujol's signature dish, the 'two moles dish, Mole Madre, Mole Nuevo',
is not to be missed: the soft tortilla, fresh from the oven, is probably the best
you have ever tasted.

Inside a 1950s bungalow in the Polanco neighbourhood, the gardens, wood-burning oven, and record player and vinyl collection lend an air of intimacy to the fine-dining restaurant Pujol. In the kitchen, celebrity chef Enrique Olvera offers two different dining options: a multi-course tasting menu in the formal dining room and a 'taco omakase' meal at the low-slung bar. Starting with street-food-inspired snacks, like a stuffed corn doughnut topped with pico de gallo (red onions and tomato salsa), or a corn crisp made of chia seeds with sea urchin, the must-try is Pujol's signature dish, the 'two moles dish, Mole Madre, Mole Nuevo', which consists of twin puddles of ground spices, nuts, fruits and chillies, mixed into bitter-rich sauces. The first one, bright red, is freshly made, and the second one, darker, has been aged for 1,000 days. The contrasting flavours make the perfect topping on the homemade tortilla.

MEXICO

Mexico City
Avenue Isaac Newton 55, Polanco, CDMX, Mexico City

**MODERN
MEXICAN**

◆ TO VISIT BEFORE YOU DIE BECAUSE

It is essential to visit the rooftop garden with the knowledgeable and wise chef Jorge Vallejo before you leave.

Off a smart-looking street in Mexico City's Polanco district, in blond-wood modern rooms with a green colour palette and a stunning green wall, Quintonil represents the new and exciting Mexican food scene in a relaxed and elegant atmosphere. Naming his restaurant after a Mexican herb, chef Jorge Vallejo gives special attention to the plant and vegetable world, as well as to the 'milpa', the traditional rotational farming method. With his wife Alejandra at the front of house, his beliefs are reflected in an earthy ten-course tasting menu that focuses on vegetables, roots and herbs, using indigenous produce and vegetables from his garden. The fresh tomato salad with Cotija cheese is as clean as precise as other highlights such as sardines in green sauce with purslane, fennel and guacamole, or the colourful panna cotta with sweetened corn crumble and mamey seed ice cream.

www.quintonil.com

— 14 —
SUD 777

MEXICO

Mexico City
Boulevard De La Luz 777,
Jardines Del Pedregal, Mexico City

**MODERN
MEXICAN**

◆ TO VISIT BEFORE YOU DIE BECAUSE

The zen ambience of this contemporary space, with its green plants and
the sound of the water flowing, is refreshing.

Sud 777, a contemporary space that merges
indoors with outdoors, is one of the sexiest
restaurants in town. The young chef Edgar
Nuñez has worked at some of the world's
top restaurants, including Noma and El
Bulli, and is currently one of the young
chefs leading the rise in Mexico. Committed
to rescuing and recontextualising
Mexican cuisine, his aim is to create his
own contemporary approach, using local
ingredients mixed with global influences.
The menu is divided into sections such as
'River and Sea', 'Heaven and Earth' and
'Mexican Coasts', made from domestically
sourced ingredients that reflect the clean,
fresh flavours of his terroir's produce
and seafood. His signature dishes include
cold vegetable soup and raspberry salad,
subtle beef tongue on inky black beans
with purslane blossoms and a salad of tiny
heirloom tomatoes with chicharrón (fried
pork skin) and minced cactus in a Cotija
cheese vinaigrette.

	Mexico City	
MEXICO	Sinaloa 141. Col. Roma Norte. Del. Cuauhtémoc C.P. 06700 CDMX	**MODERN MEXICAN**

◆ TO VISIT BEFORE YOU DIE BECAUSE

You simply must try young chef Oswaldo Oliva's cuisine, which brings back Basque influences to his native country.

The Mexican chef Oswaldo Oliva had spent 10 years at Mugaritz in the Basque country when he decided to realise his dream with his wife Elizabeth and opened Lorea ('flower' in Basque), and established it as one of the best dining experiences in Mexico City. In a two-part apartment converted into a stylish restaurant with an open kitchen, Lorea offers a creative experience using traditional European cooking techniques and local ingredients from the shores of Baja to the Yucatán peninsula. Throughout the dinner, the waiters dressed in custom-made grey shirts and blouses serve, in a choreographed performance, toasted sourdough bread topped with a thin sliver of glazed pork belly, large prawns topped with thin shavings of wild mushrooms and corn inoculated with fungus, which turns the whole cob black.

UNITED STATES

Nashville
1711 Division Street, Nashville, TN 37203

CHEF'S COUNTER

◆ TO VISIT BEFORE YOU DIE BECAUSE

You can experience the wide world of experience of chef Ryan Poli, from Japan to France, in one place.

The novel and experimental Catbird Seat is a tiny 23-seat restaurant named after the American expression meaning 'to have the upper hand'. Ryan Poli, an American chef who has trained at Noma, The French Laundry, Blue Hill at Stone Barns and El Celler de Can Roca, is the third to take the helm at this culinary incubator. At a U-shaped dining counter, Poli and his team are happy to chat with diners about dishes, techniques and ingredients while they are preparing the innovative American-based tasting menu. Diners are greeted with 'faux-reos' (Oreos biscuits filled with parmesan and porcini mushrooms) or a hot chicken that the chef has deconstructed into a single delicious bite of crispy baked chicken skin, sprinkled with a heavy coating of cayenne and paprika.

www.thecatbirdseatrestaurant.com

UNITED STATES	Nashville	MODERN AMERICAN
	37 Rutledge Street, Nashville, TN 37210	

◆ TO VISIT BEFORE YOU DIE BECAUSE

Chef Sean Brock has reinvented southern food in a Victorian setting, combining forgotten ingredients with a modern approach.

Centrally located in historic downtown Charleston, Husk is housed in a beautiful Victorian mansion, with a main dining room that retains all its vintage charm, an entrance with firewood to fuel the oven and a large board listing the craft producers that currently supply the kitchen. In the kitchen, chef Sean Brock is the one who originally prepared its menus, using locally sourced ingredients to reinvent southern food. His modern approach gives rise to fun dishes such as eggs stuffed with marinated okra and trout roe, as well as new classics like shrimp stew with Carolina gold rice and flowering basil. The restaurant is uncompromising in its commitment to local and seasonal sourcing. It works with farms to revive ancient grains and vegetables threatened with extinction, and supports producers of rare animal breeds.

husknashville.com

BLUE HILL
AT STONE BARNS

| UNITED
STATES | New York City
630 Bedford Road, Pocantico Hills,
New York, NY 10591 | FARM-TO-TABLE |

◆ TO VISIT BEFORE YOU DIE BECAUSE

Chef Dan Barber is one of the most inspiring visionaries changing the whole food world from the seeds and soils.

Blue Hill at Stone Barns is located within Stone Barns Center for Food and Agriculture, a non-profit working farm and educational centre. The restaurant is set inside a beautiful barn in Pocantico Hills, 30 miles north of New York City, and chef Dan Barber is a proponent of regenerative gastronomy; he has also set up the wastED pop-ups, making entire menus from underappreciated and underutilised ingredients. Sourcing from the surrounding fields and pastures, as well as other local farms, Blue Hill at Stone Barns highlights the abundance of the Hudson Valley, bringing thoughtful, delicious plates to the table. In the elegant dining room, with its double-height ceilings, diners taste a menu of approximately 30 bites and courses, while an accompanying harvest journal and the restaurant's team serve as guides to the meal. The procession of dishes may include a tiny beef-heart tart under a stack of grissini 'hay', weeds from land and sea to be grasped with the fingers, and an array of lettuce heads fresh from the farm.

— 19 —
CHEF'S TABLE AT BROOKLYN FARE

UNITED STATES	New York City	CHEF'S COUNTER
	431 West 37th Street, New York, NY 10018, inside Brooklyn Fare market	

◆ TO VISIT BEFORE YOU DIE BECAUSE

This is a wonderful opportunity to experience an interactive moment with the chef, with no note-taking or photography allowed.

Originally from Mexico, chef César Ramirez previously worked at Danube and Bouley in New York. In contrast to traditional fine-dining restaurants, his Chef's Table at Brooklyn Fare is located in the annex of an upmarket grocer's shop in Brooklyn; it has only 18 seats available, with the aim of fostering an intimate, interactive atmosphere. With no note-taking or photography allowed, the experience of a 20-plus course tasting menu is inspired by the best sushi restaurants in Japan, with a procession of exquisite single bites, such as Japanese snapper with olive-oil ponzu sauce and crispy leeks, kumamoto oyster over a gelée made of oyster liquor or king crab with yuzu marmalade. The Chef's Table has no alcohol licence, but has glasses for every style of wine and an attractive ice bin in which diners can store their bottles with no corkage fee.

www.brooklynfare.com/pages/chefs-table

— 20 —
ELEVEN MADISON PARK

UNITED
STATES

New York City
11 Madison Avenue, New York, NY 10010

MODERN
AMERICAN

◆ TO VISIT BEFORE YOU DIE BECAUSE

In this former bank in a landmark Art Deco building you can mingle with New York's most stylish crowd.

With its high ceilings and hushed grandeur, Eleven Madison Park feels like a sanctuary, with its clean, updated aesthetic featuring cobalt blue mohair banquettes, terrazzo tiling and a blue painting by artist Rita Ackermann. Swiss-born chef Daniel Humm started working in kitchens at the age of 14, and earned his first Michelin star at 24. Becoming executive chef at Eleven Madison Park in 2006 when the restaurant was owned by Danny Meyer's Union Square Hospitality Group, and took on co-ownership a few years later with the charismatic Will Guidara, who runs the front of the house. Humm has a minimal design aesthetic in his creations, and his sophisticated cooking and plating have earned him three stars from Michelin. On the menu, he has introduced an iconic lavender and honey dry-aged Duclair duck roasted with cabbage and pear, as well as a savoury New York cheesecake made from smoked sturgeon, anointed with asparagus and a mountain of caviar. For those looking to experience a shorter meal, the bar offers an abbreviated five-course tasting menu instead of the dining room's eight to ten plates.

— 21 —
THE GRILL

New York City

The Seagram Building 99 East 52nd Street,
New York, NY 10022

TRADITIONAL
AMERICAN

◆ TO VISIT BEFORE YOU DIE BECAUSE

Here you can enjoy the bustling 50s atmosphere of the greatest dining room in
New York City.

The Grill is a historic American chophouse set in midtown New York that has become an institution. The 60-year-old venue's immortal design and architectural grandeur have been recently revamped by the chef Mario Carbone, who has refurbished this classic to an era when things were still intricate and elegant. The past is a key component of the restaurant's formula, particularly in the main dining room, evoking the 1940s and 1950s with high style: Zac Posen-clad waiters, Julian Schnabel's artworks on the walls and fancy Caesar salads on the plates. The menu offers extensive tableside preparations, reflecting the style of service favoured half a century ago: carving, saucing and flambéing from a quartet of gleaming, floor-roaming trolleys. The classics of the house include spit-roasted prime rib carved at the tableside and Dover sole meunière skinned and boned in front of diners; there is also a duck press on display, along with garlic, tomatoes and herbs.

| UNITED STATES | New York City
10 Columbus Circle, Time Warner Center, 4th Floor,
New York, NY 10019 | JAPANESE OMAKASE |

◆ TO VISIT BEFORE YOU DIE BECAUSE
It is one of the most refined and gracious omakase experiences outside Japan.

In New York City, where there is the highest concentration of Michelin-starred Japanese restaurants outside of Japan itself, Masa is the one that stands out. Sushi master Masa Takayama was apprenticed under the direction of Sugiyama Toshiaki at Tokyo's well-respected Ginza Sushi-ko before following his boyhood dream to travel to the USA. Located on the fourth floor of the Time Warner Center at 10 Columbus Circle in New York, Masa, with its minimalistic decor, is of course a place to eat, but above all it is a sensory experience. Connaisseurs will ask to be seated at the sushi bar in one of the ten oversized leather chairs over the pristine hinoki wood table, where the chef creates an unforgettable dining experience through each carefully crafted piece of sushi in an omakase menu, which translates as 'I'll leave it to you.' Sushi is served lukewarm, each individual grain of its sticky rice balls contrasts in temperature with the cold fish that gives it a creamy and rich texture. This is surely the reason why the late chef Anthony Bourdain said that Masa Takayama has the best sushi rice – the true determinant of great sushi – in the world.

— 23 —
MOMOFUKU KO

UNITED STATES

New York City
8 Extra Place, New York, NY 10003

CHEF'S COUNTER

◆ TO VISIT BEFORE YOU DIE BECAUSE

This is the place to go to taste the subtle, refreshing shaved razor clams in pineapple broth, dashi and basil seed.

Ko's creator, Korean-American chef David Chiang, is an iconoclast who has changed fine dining with his chef-delivered tasting menus: when he first opened in the original Noodle Bar space in East Village, only a dozen diners could fit around the kitchen on the uncomfortable wooden stools for a tasting menu that included syrup-soaked lychees straight from the tin, served under a rain of frozen cured foie gras. In 2018 Ko moved to an upgraded space and became a model of contemporary fine dining, serving one of New York City's most elegant and exquisite tasting menus thanks to the chef Sean Alex Gray and general manager Su Ruiz. With music by The Who as the soundtrack, the main dining space showcases huge glass refrigerators with dry-aged steaks, plates and kitchenware, and a stack of labelled spices with bright colours. But in all this playful design and high-end equipment, the real fun to be had at Ko is in watching the chefs wearing black baseball caps, and chatting easily with customers while they grill dishes in the middle of the stage. Look out for chef Gray sliding a buttery potato purée tickled with fermented radish and caviar, or a soft chickpea purée paired with sea urchin and hozon, over the wide, gleaming walnut counter.

ko.momofuku.com

— 24 —
LE COUCOU

New York City
138 Lafayette Street, New York, NY 10013

TRADITIONAL
FRENCH

◆ TO VISIT BEFORE YOU DIE BECAUSE

This is the place to feel the disruptive experience of eating traditional French cooking in a splendid setting in the heart of Manhattan.

At the entrance, wood planters filled with climbing jasmine and roses frame the doorway, and a bright neon Le Coucou sign featuring the playful outline of a bird sets the scene. Inside, there are high ceilings, candlelit tables and long blue crushed-velvet banquettes. French-trained chef Daniel Rose, from Spring, and bistro La Bourse et La Vie and Chez La Vieille in Paris, delivers a true tribute to French cuisine in the grand, loft-like space. The menu offers simple and seasonal cuisine with impeccably sourced ingredients: whole rabbit, buckwheat-fried eel with curry vinaigrette, and a to-die-for mousse au chocolat, all prepared in the open kitchen from where Rose can watch his guests dining. Book a window table and watch the glinting towers of New York to remind you that you are not actually in Paris.

lecoucou.com

— 25 —
ATOMIX

New York City
104 East 30th Street, New York, NY 10016

◆ TO VISIT BEFORE YOU DIE BECAUSE
Here you can experience a whole meal translated in poetic words all through the Korean fine-dining tasting menu.

Right in the speakeasies trend, Atomix is tucked inside the foyer of an apartment building on East 30th Street. On the lower level, the chef Junghyun Park, who also operates Atoboy with his wife, serves a multi-course tasting menu of innovative Korean cuisine in a futuristic dining room, where geometric couches are scattered around the stone floor. Instead of receiving a menu, diners collect a series of cards explaining the ten courses, made of deep-fried langoustine with creamed uni and nasturtium, and caviar over delicate baby artichokes and fresh cheese curds.

UNITED STATES	New York City	MODERN MEDITERRANEAN
	47 East Houston Street, New York, NY 10012	

◆ TO VISIT BEFORE YOU DIE BECAUSE

Mattos was the first to change the fine dining scene in NYC giving it a more relaxed and layed back vibe, which even attracts Barack Obama as a regular.

Located up a few steps off East Houston Street, Estela is an interesting part of the Manhattan scene. With its marble bar and exposed-brick walls, and its lively and humble vibe, Estela is the kind of place you will love when you are sick of overthought food. Uruguay-born chef Ignacio Mattos has spent some time at Alice Waters' Chez Panisse in California. His philosophy is about providing Mediterranean-inspired food through basic dishes with exceptional tastes. There are no tasting menus, just a range of items to share on the table, such as burrata cheese with salsa verde, plump folded omelette hiding a creamed oyster tang of sea urchins, and an amazing arroz negro with squid.

www.estelanyc.com

	Panama City	
PANAMA	Final de la Calle 50	MODERN
	4to Local a mano izquierda, Panama City	PANAMANIAN

◆ TO VISIT BEFORE YOU DIE BECAUSE

Maito's chef and creator, Mario Castrellón, was the first to plant the seeds of a new Panamanian cuisine with a modern vision.

Maito's chef and creator, Mario Castrellón, was the first to plant the seeds of a new Panamanian cuisine with a modern vision, using ingredients that, while recognisably national, have not traditionally gone into sophisticated cuisine. Modern versions of the classics include exotic *flor eléctrica* (a flowering herb that grows on the slopes of the nation's highest volcano), *carimañola* stuffed pies and slow-roasted pork with Panamanian tortilla. The tasting menu is a tropical journey through Caribbean, indigenous, Asian, Creole, Afro-Antillean and American cuisine that expresses Panama's multicultural culinary identity. Castrellón constantly researches native products and visits producers, artisans and indigenous communities and he has his own organic farm. He has also begun a movement of young chefs looking to foster a Panamanian identity on the plate.

www.maitopanama.com

— 28 —
THE RANCH
AT ROCK CREEK

UNITED
STATES

Philipsburg
79 Carriage House Lane, Philipsburg, MT 59858

MODERN
AMERICAN

◆ TO VISIT BEFORE YOU DIE BECAUSE

Diners can taste Montana alfalfa in the grass-fed beef or wild flowers in
a Sapphire Mountain honey vinaigrette.

Diners can embrace the Wild West spirit at The Ranch at Rock Creek, an estate in Montana covering 6,600 acres near the Beaverhead-Deerlodge National Forest and the Anaconda-Pintler Wilderness area. At this unique ranch that offers a luxury country experience, guests can try their hands at fly fishing, horse riding, shooting, archery or a ropes course. The ranch's cuisine tells a story about wildlife, herbs and harvest with regionally and locally sourced organic ingredients prepared on a wood fire grill or in a Dutch oven. Diners arrive in the early evening in the Great Room to enjoy artisan cocktails made with local herbs, and then step in to dine by the fire and share tales under the big sky.

IN SITU

| UNITED
STATES | San Francisco
MOMA, 151 Third Street,
San Francisco, CA 94103 | MODERN
INTERNATIONAL |

◆ TO VISIT BEFORE YOU DIE BECAUSE

The most iconic dishes from some of the world's best chefs can be tasted in this arty environment.

In the neutral minimalist design of In Situ, located in the San Francisco Museum of Modern Art, the colourful chefs' creations look like masterpieces. Chef-operator Corey Lee – San Francisco's 2017 James Beard Award winner, for his work at Benu – curates the menu by selecting top chefs around the world who are creating innovative food and are having a significant impact on the industry. In so doing, Lee gathers a unique collection of iconic dishes. Lee has trained his cooks to work closely with the recipes' originators to faithfully replicate the technique and presentation of the 100 menu items, which could be signature dishes or new creations, imagined exclusively for the place. Paralleling the explanations that often accompany artworks in a gallery, the folded menu looks like a guide to an exhibition of works on temporary loan, showing the birthplaces of

the 15 dishes. A key in the right margin gives each dish's ingredients, its originator's name and location, and the year it was invented. On the reverse there is a quote from the originating chef and a curator-like appraisal of the significance of the restaurant. Rotating seasonally, the menu ensures that diners will always have new 'exhibits' to sample. It might feature the guinea fowl larb salad Chiang Mai with its tasty blend of meat and herbs created in 1999 by David Thompson at Nahm in Bangkok, or the artfully subtle Forest created in 2011 by Mauro Colagreco at Mirazur in Menton, with wild mushrooms, tender green stems and a fuchsia sweet pea flower scattered on and around a bed of quinoa risotto.

insitu.sfmoma.org

	San Francisco	
UNITED STATES	22 Hawthorne Street, San Francisco, CA 94105	**FUSION**

◆ TO VISIT BEFORE YOU DIE BECAUSE

The three-star Corey Lee foie gras xiao long bao – Shanghaiese foie gras soup dumpling – is not to be missed.

In the sleek, minimalist grey dining room with bare-wood tables, in the SoMa district of downtown San Francisco, Benu has quickly won widespread critical acclaim for its refined approach to cooking. Born in Korea, chef Corey Lee moved at an early age to the USA and went on to work in several fine-dining establishments (The French Laundry, Guy Savoy and Alain Senderens, among others). The menu at Benu reflects his own globetrotting history, blending influences from Asia, Europe and the USA into a bright 16- to 20-course menu. The signatures include a flash-fried cigarette of eel wrapped in Moroccan feuille de brick with crème fraîche, home-made tofu with pumpkin juice and black truffle, and faux shark's fin soup, made by treating the broth with hydrocolloids.

www.benusf.com

— 31 —
SAISON

San Francisco
178 Townsend Street, San Francisco, CA 94107

MODERN
AMERICAN

◆ TO VISIT BEFORE YOU DIE BECAUSE

Here you can try 'Liquid Toast', a glazed sea urchin served on crusty bread soaked in a rich sauce and dusted with a powder of river vegetables.

Saison is America's most modern iteration of a casual ultra-luxury restaurant. Young executive chef and co-owner Joshua Skenes attended the French Culinary Institute in New York and worked with Jean-Georges Vongerichten before starting a Sunday-night-only pop-up in a former stable. Becoming permanent, Saison moved to an elegant 1800s building that once housed the California Electric Light Company, where Skenes still uses unique techniques from cooking traditions around the world and weaves them into a personal mosaic. At the exclusive 18 covers table, with 1980s or 1990s rock classics playing in the background, diners begin with a tea of Meyer lemon and herbs, followed by a splash of champagne with caviar-smoked sturgeon belly and gelée, before moving on to pickled horse mackerel on thin toast with crème fraîche and roasted abalone.

www.saisonsf.com

— 32 —
BORAGÓ

Santiago
Av. Nueva Costanera 3467, Vitacura, Santiago

◆ TO VISIT BEFORE YOU DIE BECAUSE

It is an opportunity to understand chef Rodolfo Guzmán's inspiration from the indigenous people of Chile, from recipes and techniques that were used centuries ago.

Boragó is a word invented by owner-chef Rodolfo Guzmán, reflecting his passion for creating dishes from lesser-known wild ingredients gathered from all over Chile. Guzmán wants to understand human behaviour through food and discover how it can help us lead healthier lives. In his restaurant's interior, with its concrete floor and wooden tables inspired by both the pure and rough aspects of nature, Guzmán's cuisine uses local traditions and ingredients from the sea, forests, valleys and mountains. Marked by the seasons, his cooking reclaims native preparations in a way that is untamed, rustic and indigenous, for example mixing conger eel with the sweet-onion taste of sea starflowers or the milk of cows, goats and donkeys in a radical take on the classic tres leches dessert.

DOM

São Paulo

Rua Barão de Capanema, 549, Jardins, São Paulo, SP

◆ TO VISIT BEFORE YOU DIE BECAUSE

Here you can hear chef Alex Atala's stories about the small farmers, riverside communities and regional producers he visits throughout the year.

Located in the neighbourhood of Jardins in São Paulo, restaurant DOM's name was inspired by the Benedictine motto 'Deo optimo maximo', which translates as 'To God, the best and greatest', indicating the places where weary pilgrims would eat and rest. In a stylish interior with high ceilings and decorated in earth colours, chef Alex Atala has been a pioneer in the promotion of Aboriginal cuisine, bringing local Brazilian produce to the forefront of the international gastronomic scene. He has focused his research on the Amazon region, which he visits a few times a year with anthropologists to better understand the local people and their culture. Giving preference to ingredients grown by small farmers, riverside communities and regional producers, promoting local culture is something that is always present in this restaurant's menu. Atala brings traditional ingredients like manioc, heart of palm and pirarucu (freshwater fish) together with European techniques learnt from his travels to create complex contemporary dishes, including brilliant combinations such as mushrooms and Brazilian honey, and yogurt snow with green papaya.

domrestaurante.com.br/pt-br/home.html

— 34 —
HARTWOOD

MEXICO

Tulum

Carretera Tulum Boca Paila 7.6Km, 77780 Tulum

OPEN FIRE

◆ TO VISIT BEFORE YOU DIE BECAUSE

You can admire the wonderful job Hartwood has made of staying true to Tulum's vibe with only the open sky for its roof and its paradise-like setting.

Chef Eric Werner and his wife Mya Henry were on holiday in Tulum when they had the idea to ditch the fast-paced restaurant life in New York and decided to set up Hartwood from scratch. In the open-air restaurant, on the jungle side of Tulum, solar panels are the source of sustainable energy and a wood-burning oven is used to prepare the Mexican-inspired dishes. The place prides itself on having no menu; instead, there are daily options based on whatever is available from nearby ranches and farms, featuring locally sourced ingredients only. Chef Werner brings food back to basics and showcases exquisite products by slow roasting and open-fire cooking meat, such as the intense pork ribs, or serving the colourful jicama salad with mint crema, and the tuna ceviche with ruby red tiger's milk marinade. Hartwood's dreamy ambience, with its gravel floor and palm-shaded outdoor setting, has made it one of Tulum's most popular and in-demand dining rooms.

www.hartwoodtulum.com

— 35 —
KADEAU

Åkirkeby

DENMARK

Baunevej 18, Vestre Sømark,
Pedersker, 3720 Åkirkeby

**MODERN
SCANDINAVIAN**

◆ TO VISIT BEFORE YOU DIE BECAUSE

The Kadeau project is much more than just a restaurant: it is a love affair with the homeland and a company based on friendship, which you can feel in all the details, from the atmosphere to the table.

As an early exponent of the New Nordic movement, chef Nicolai Nørregaard opened the original Kadeau with Rasmus and Magnus Kofoed on the tiny Baltic island of Bornholm. Attached to their native island, the friends chose a lovely white converted seaside shack by the sandy coast to establish their magical place and serve a creative cuisine made out of wild coastal herbs and homegrown vegetables. The poetic 20-course tasting menu is based on nature and locally farmed ingredients, including fresh oysters paired with hemp and wrapped in a kale leaf, and fermented flower petals set with preserved berries and nasturtium leaves. The team returns to Kadeau Bornholm every year during the summer season and cooks at the Copenhagen Kadeau for the rest of the year.

www.kadeau.dk

ITALY	**Alba** Piazza Risorgimento 4, 12051 Alba (CN)	MODERN ITALIAN

TO VISIT BEFORE YOU DIE BECAUSE

It is a must to visit the region during the white truffle festival (October and November) to taste the wonderful products of the Barolo region of Piedmont, with its rolling green hills and its ochre-walled towns.

Set on the first floor of the medieval square in Alba, the three-Michelin-star Piazza Duomo is led by chef Enrico Crippa. As soon as you enter the place, you will notice that the setting is rather unusual: a wide open room in soft pink, decorated with painted vine leaves by the Italian artist Francesco Clemente, who was inspired by the local landscape. Crippa has access to the very best of produce thanks to his restaurant's location in the food paradise of Piedmont, renowned for its cheeses, hazelnuts, grand wines and truffles, as well as his own garden of five hectares with plenty of vegetables, where he finds inspiration for creating his menus. The parade of snacks is extraordinary, featuring olives that are not in fact real ones, but small balls stuffed with a tartare of prawn. Highlights include the intricate 'Salad 21, 31, 41, 51', which references the varying number of seasonal ingredients put in a glass bowl containing a dash of broth, while 'Panna Cotta Matisse', inspired by the master chef Gualtiero Marchesi, is a colourful mosaic of seasonal fruits and vegetables.

— 37 —
DE KAS

THE NETHERLANDS

Amsterdam
Kamerlingh Onneslaan 3,
1097 DE Amsterdam

FARM-TO-TABLE

◆ TO VISIT BEFORE YOU DIE BECAUSE
The beautiful greenhouse and its splendid gardens alone make a visit more than worth your while.

Chef Gert-Jan Hageman, the founder and head grower, is a pioneering farm-to-table supporter who took over this restaurant and nursery in Amsterdam. After achieving a Michelin star at Vermeer restaurant, he went on sabbatical. When he came back, he was determined not only to save a 1926 nursery in Amsterdam East from demolition, but also to grow organic vegetables. In the gorgeous former greenhouse, with its airy high ceilings and vast windows, guests can enjoy the local, organic and vege-centric menu, with most ingredients coming from the on-site nursery or nearby farm.

— 38 —
THE JANE

BELGIUM

Antwerp
Paradeplein 1, 2018 Antwerp

MODERN
EUROPEAN

◆ TO VISIT BEFORE YOU DIE BECAUSE

In this converted church you can have a unique gourmet experience, with loud music, exciting cocktails and the smell of incense.

Located in the former chapel of the nineteenth-century Military Hospital in Antwerp, The Jane is the gastronomic establishment of business partners head chef Nick Bril and chef Sergio Herman, that offers a unique combination of top-notch cuisine made accessible for a broad audience. Acclaimed designer Piet Boon ensured the restaurant's design together with various artists, making The Jane a real gem where the vision of a restaurant in which 'fine dining meets rock-n-roll' is realised.

Regarding food as a religion, the chefs' team works in an open kitchen where the altar of the chapel once stood. Downstairs, colourful culinary creations are served at the tables, surrounded by decorative details: stained-glass windows with tattoo inspirations and a gigantic, neon-shaped skull serving as examples. On the mezzanine level, in the Upper Room Bar, the DJ plays music, while the patrons enjoy tapas, cocktails and a plunging view of the colossal, custom-made chandelier.

— 39 —
LA CHASSAGNETTE

Arles

FRANCE

Mas de la Chassagnette
Chemin du Sambuc, Arles

FARM-TO-TABLE

◆ TO VISIT BEFORE YOU DIE BECAUSE

Here you can have the most unforgettable lunch at the long wooden tables on the vine-shaded terrace.

Located a few minutes away from Arles, the Michelin-starred restaurant La Chassagnette is a tribute to nature and the art of cooking. In the two-hectare garden that flourishes on the soil of the Rhône delta, chef Armand Arnal draws his inspiration from nature's subtle and essential harmony, waiting for the ideal harvesting time for the vegetables that he serves on the vine-shaded terrace. Saint-Gilles pink and herb-scented lamb comes from 20 miles away, while sea bream from the Mediterranean Sea is cooked in fennel juice and an emerald-green emulsion of herbs.

www.chassagnette.fr

SPAIN

Atxondo

Asador Etxebarri, Plaza de San Juan 1,
48291 Atxondo, Bizkaia

**OPEN
FIRE**

◆ TO VISIT BEFORE YOU DIE BECAUSE

You will taste the cuisine of the best chefs' ultimate cooking mentor, chef Victor Arguinzoniz.

The experience begins in the town of Atxondo in the Basque region of Spain, with its old church whose bell tolls the hours, a small square with a water fountain, and a couple of sheep in their paddock. Inside the restaurant, the decor reflects this rustic setting and mixes it with elements of contemporary art. Chef Victor Arguinzoniz is self-taught and has only ever worked in his own kitchen. He is one of the most respected and inspiring chefs of his generation using exclusively the fire, live coal, and embers from oak and grapevines to cook the very best of the region's ingredients. Considered as the chefs' ultimate mentor, he has invented his own unique technique, designing adjustable-height grills to coax the maximum flavour from each ingredient. Alongside his 15-course tasting menu, the cooking and flavours are what are called perfect: the steak garnished with smoked butter is barely touched by the grill, with a thin crust caramelised on the outside and a ruby-red inside, and roasted gambas are juicy and melt in the mouth.

asadoretxebarri.com

DISFRUTAR

SPAIN	Barcelona	MODERN SPANISH
	C/Villarroel 163, Barcelona 08036	

◆ TO VISIT BEFORE YOU DIE BECAUSE

This is where you can enjoy the spheres that look exactly like olives but which are filled with mandarin flower essence, a famous dish inherited from El Bulli in Catalonia.

Disfrutar (meaning 'enjoy' in Spanish) is a beautiful Mediterranean restaurant in Barcelona, with clay ceramics and a white dining room that flows out onto the terrace, referencing the small fishing villages of Catalonia. Oriol Castro, Eduard Xatruch and Mateu Casañas were, for many years, head chefs of the famous El Bulli, the restaurant from which Ferran Adrià and his team branded a worldwide culinary revolution until it closed in 2011. The multi-course tasting menus announce one theatrical avant-garde dish after another, dizzying the senses and leaving diners with smiles on their faces: for example, transparent tubes of 'macaroni', made from gelatine, tossed in truffle and parmesan foam, and a deconstructed whisky tart, which involves washing your hands in whisky and sniffing them as you eat.

SPAIN	**Barcelona** Carrer Sepúlveda 38–40, on the corner with Entença, 08015, Barcelona	MODERN SPANISH

◆ TO VISIT BEFORE YOU DIE BECAUSE

Here you can live an El Bulli revival through an interactive experience.

Albert Adrià, brother of world-famous chef Ferran Adrià and former El Bulli chef, is one of Barcelona's most successful restaurateurs. At Enigma, he intends to recreate what his brother's experience would be today. Located in a majestic space that combines Japanese minimalism with vintage science fiction, Enigma is definitely not a conventional restaurant. Once the reservation is confirmed, diners receive a code to enter the restaurant where they will discover the 40 dishes of the tasting menu combining influences from around the world, including Japan, Spain, Korea, and Brazil, such as squid cut to mimic sushi rice, blanketed with coconut fat, a ring of nori topped with Schrenki caviar, or raspberry pods with dill and sour cream, all served on unusual plates. Diners do not remain static during the unique experience: they move through the seven distinct dining spaces, each one with its own theme, from La Plantxa, featuring a teppanyaki-inspired set-up with a flat-top grill, to the 41º cocktail bar, where bartender Marc Álvarez serves marvellous concoctions.

SPAIN

Barcelona
Av. de Mistral 54, 08015 Barcelona

MODERN MEXICAN

◆ TO VISIT BEFORE YOU DIE BECAUSE

Hoja Santa is the perfect place to discover the savour of cactus nopal juice mixed with an oyster, pineapple, lemon and olive oil.

Named after an aromatic herb with heart-shaped leaves that grows in the tropical parts of Mexico, Hoja Santa is one of the restaurants opened by Albert Adrià that takes us to the country's haute cuisine. Located in the same building as the taqueria Niño Viejo in the Parallel neighbourhood of Barcelona. Mexican chef Paco Méndez uses recipes from the different regions, showcasing the very best of what contemporary Mexican cuisine has to offer, thanks to his former experience at El Bulli and at Tickets. Expect diversity, the complexity of layers of tastes and contrasting textures from a wonderful tasting set menu, including the Tequila cloud, a new version of Ferran Adrià's olive, filled with a vivid mixture of salsa verde, lime juice, Tabasco and coriander, or an oyster with cactus juice, pineapple, lemon and olive oil.

www.hojasanta.es

— 44 —
KOY SHUNKA

SPAIN

Barcelona
C/ Copons 7, 08002 Barcelona

MODERN
JAPANESE

◆ TO VISIT BEFORE YOU DIE BECAUSE

At Koy Shunka in Spain, local products are prepared in an inventive Japanese way.

Koy Shunka is a gourmet Japanese restaurant in the historic district of Barrio Gótico in Barcelona. Born in Toyota in Japan, chef Hideki Matsuhisa was educated at a young age in the art of Japanese cuisine at his father's restaurant, Nobu. Koy Shunka's main selling point is the produce, which is precisely cut and cooked, with purity and simplicity. The chef's work is, despite appearances, distinctly of Barcelona: the ingredients that Matsuhisa chooses, such as white asparagus from Gava or eel from Delta del Ebro, showcase the region's producers. The highlights of the show are the nigiris: they come directly from the hands of the chef, with precision and control, to arrive on your plate with a buttery texture and no change in temperature.

— 45 —
ERNST

GERMANY

Berlin
Gerichtstraße 54, 13347 Berlin

FARM-TO-TABLE

◆ TO VISIT BEFORE YOU DIE BECAUSE
Ernst offers an interactive farm-to-table experience at a counter with
the buzzing young Berlin chefs.

Ernst is a 12-seat restaurant in the Wedding area in Berlin that has recently been listed as one of the best new restaurants featuring refined farm-to-table cuisine. Seated along the counter in front of the kitchen, guests can watch the team throughout the process of cooking the 25-course meal, while the five chefs, anchored by Dylan Watson-Brawn, share stories about the farmers, winemakers and artisans. After positions in Copenhagen and New York, Watson-Brawn moved to Berlin and began to cook in his apartment, before creating Ernst. Building his menu on pure taste, most of the single-vegetable plates are 'radically fresh' as Watson-Brawn works closely with regional organic farms to realise his vision.

SPAIN	Bilbao Av. Abandoibarra 2, 48001 Bilbao, Bizkaia	MODERN SPANISH

◆ TO VISIT BEFORE YOU DIE BECAUSE

At Nerua you can experience innovative Basque cuisine in a sleek, contemporary setting, while sitting in front of Jeff Koons's Puppy sculpture.

Housed in the legendary Guggenheim Museum in Bilbao, overlooking the river, Michelin-starred Nerua serves innovative Basque cuisine in a sleek, contemporary setting with fresh white walls and swirl-backed chairs. Chef Josean Alija's story is not a typical one: he started his culinary journey while very young, at age 14, and then in his early 20s suffered a life-threatening accident that left him in a coma for 21 days. He returned to food with a strong desire to rediscover it like no one ever before. All his audacious dishes are served on simple white plates with just two or three ingredients, using Mediterranean produce such as anchovies, duck, cod and chocolate, to which he is not afraid to add unusual flashes of inspiration, like green coffee essence, pumpkin seed praline and 'spicy marzipan sand'.

— 47 —
THE FAT DUCK

UNITED KINGDOM	Bray High Street, Bray, Berkshire SL6 2AQ	MODERN INVENTIVE

◆ TO VISIT BEFORE YOU DIE BECAUSE

The Fat Duck has become a legendary place to experience a fabulous fantasy meal with unexpected crazy dishes.

In the village of Bray, west of London, in a tiny cottage seating about 40 guests, chef Heston Blumenthal's singular restaurant has been raising smiles for more than 20 years. Blumenthal became famous with unusual culinary creations such as crab ice cream and snail porridge, and, with dishes that pickle the mind, his idea is to devise a multisensory experience in which all that you touch, hear, smell and feel has an effect. There is nothing ordinary about dining at The Fat Duck, from the booking process to the petit fours, from the innovative dish presentations to the original flavour combinations. In place of a regular menu, there is a map that might take you on a trip to the seaside, which starts with the journey to the coast, continues with a visit to the beach and a walk in the woods, then ends with dinner, followed by bedtime and dreams. And, of course, with the food, nothing is quite as it seems: the ingredients of a Waldorf salad turn into an ice cream; a gold watch vanishes in hot broth to create a soup; and a weightless beetroot and horseradish macaroon disappears on the tongue.

www.thefatduck.co.uk

	Cadzand-Bad	
THE NETHERLANDS	Pure C / Strandhotel, Boulevard de Wielingen 49, 4506 JK Cadzand-Bad	**FUSION**

◆ TO VISIT BEFORE YOU DIE BECAUSE

You will admire the seaside landscape while sipping the home-made alcohol 'Hierbas de las Dunas', concocted with local herbs.

Located on the beach of Cadzand in the Netherlands, Pure C is a concept from chef Sergio Herman (previously chef of the legendary three-star Oud Sluis). In the interior designed in white with natural wood, brown seats and blue pillows, another world unfolds in front of the North Sea panoramic view. Chef Syrco Bakker is one of the Netherlands' most promising chefs, who has worked at Gordon Ramsay, De Librije and Oud Sluis. At Pure C he brings together Zeeland and exotic Indonesian accents. His dishes strike a balance between playfulness and complexity, primarily using fish and seafood that his suppliers catch in the North Sea right outside the restaurant, combined with locally grown herbs and vegetables. The seaweed and oysters from Zeeland are served with crisp rocket and sea buckthorn, and the mackerel starter comes in three preparations: in a steamy bun with mackerel and ginger; in a salad 'Gado gado' with tofu and cream of peanut; and in a preparation with soya, ginger, daikon and lemongrass. As in each of Sergio Herman's restaurants, an important part of Pure C's philosophy and strength are the great cocktails like 'Rose, shiso, hoisin and sour plum', 'Ras el hanout', 'Tomato, pomegranate', 'Grapefruit, fennel and Champagne' or 'Wheatgrass, Pure C spices, tarragon'.

— 49 —
GERANIUM

DENMARK

Copenhagen
Per Henrik Lings Allé 4, 8.,
2100 Copenhagen

**MODERN
SCANDINAVIAN**

◆ TO VISIT BEFORE YOU DIE BECAUSE

You will enjoy the stunning views on Copenhagen while discovering the 'razor clam shells' made from dough and coloured with squid ink.

On the eighth floor of Denmark's national football stadium in Copenhagen, this futurist dining room has stunning views of the Fælledparken, with glimpses of the city's rooftops. Danish-born Rasmus Kofoed is one of the most acclaimed Nordic chefs, and has won all three medal levels at the highest competition for professional chefs, the Bocuse d'Or. His cuisine explores nature's perpetual changes and beauty through colourful and dynamic techniques inspired by his childhood. Through his 20-plus course Universe menu of artfully plated dishes that changes with the seasons, head into the wild with crisp seaweed crackers, a candied carrot shell filled with orange sea buckthorn foam and Jerusalem artichoke leaves served with a creamy walnut oil and rye vinegar emulsion.

— 50 —
RELAE

DENMARK

Copenhagen
Jægersborggade 41, 2200 Copenhagen

**MODERN
SCANDINAVIAN**

◆ TO VISIT BEFORE YOU DIE BECAUSE

You would experience a well-flavoured menu based on organic vegetables from chef Christian Puglisi's own farm.

Christian Puglisi, the Italo-Norwegian chef who was raised in Denmark, was highly influenced by chef Rene Redzepi during his time as sous chef at Noma. Puglisi has recently launched his organic farm, where every morning a team of chefs collects vegetables and milk that they take back to his various restaurant kitchens in Copenhagen: Relae, Manfreds, BÆST and Mirabelle. Located in Nørrebro district, Relae is characterised by a more accessible and simplistic approach than the classic fine-dining model, with a laid-back atmosphere and a bustling open kitchen. From the drawers housing cutlery, the diners discover a written menu featuring the cutting-edge cooking of vegetables, through simple dishes maximising the flavour of just a few ingredients: for example, Jerusalem artichoke mousse with passionfruit and coffee, or fried salsify with salsify purée and bergamot.

DENMARK	Copenhagen	MODERN
	Kongens Nytorv 8, 1050 Copenhagen	SCANDINAVIAN

◆ TO VISIT BEFORE YOU DIE BECAUSE

Chef Bo Bech travels the world to create a visionary cuisine with smart and audacious ingredient pairings.

Well known in his home country as the fearsome TV host of Denmark's answer to Kitchen Nightmares, chef Bo Bech is a trailblazer of the Copenhagen food scene. He first made his name in Denmark's food-obsessed capital at Restaurant Paustian, where he won a Michelin star, before setting up Geist in 2011. But Bech is more than that. He is a man of genius and incredible taste. At Geist, located right by Kongens Nytorv square in the city centre, in an intimate dark interior with concrete floors warmed at night by the flicker of candlelight, Bech decided not to provide a set menu, but instead presents a selection of 30 dishes, to be shared and most of all experienced. Based on impeccable Scandinavian produce, the creations might look simple, but do not be fooled by their appearance: they have been definitely deeply conceptualised by Bech's genius and worldwide food experiences. His signature creation of thin layers of avocado with caviar and almond oil, for example, has even filled up a whole chapter of his new book.

restaurantgeist.dk

— 52 —
NOMA

DENMARK

Copenhagen
Refshalevej 96, 1432 Copenhagen K

**MODERN
SCANDINAVIAN**

◆ TO VISIT BEFORE YOU DIE BECAUSE

You can sip a unique koji-fermented barley milk in the green house, before being welcomed loudly by the whole team gathered when you enter the dining room. At the end, if you are lucky, you can have a private visit to the kitchen and labs with chef René Redzépi himself, the most brilliant food leader of our time.

Noma has changed the history of world cuisine over the past decade. Inventing a Nordic cuisine based on the purity and seasonality of the wild foods and traditional products of the region, the restaurant's influence has spread beyond the fine-dining sphere, and is largely responsible for all the foraged, pickled and dried ingredients you can taste on menus around the world. Recently, Noma has reopened in a new space: a rebuilt bunker inspired by a traditional Scandinavian farmstead. The kitchen has glass ceilings so that the chefs get to see daylight, while the main dining room is a soothing oak cocoon around which there will be greenhouses, rooftop gardens, a sauna and vegetable plots, eventually. The food is prepared by chef René Redzépi and his young international team based on three seasons a year: seafood from January to June, vegetables from June to early autumn, and game through to December. On the tables laid with finely handmade ceramics, the 16 courses of the seafood menu are composed of fish freshly caught from the waters around the Faroe Islands, such as sea urchin with beach rose and pumpkin-seed, venus clams and dried sea cucumber ovaries.

	Errenteria	
SPAIN	Aldura Aldea 20, 20100 Errenteria, Gipuzkoa	**MODERN SPANISH**

◆ TO VISIT BEFORE YOU DIE BECAUSE

You will be surprised by dishes that make sounds and appetisers that melt in your mouth.

The setting of Mugaritz, in the Basque hills outside San Sebastián, is spectacular: a verdant postcard of the comparatively unknown landscape of northern Spain. Like his great mentor and pioneer of molecular gastronomy Ferran Adrià, chef Andoni Luis Aduriz's philosophy is to balance his theatrical instincts with technical cooking, and to touch all of the senses by playing with perceptions. There is no menu at Mugaritz, but instead there is a sequence of up to 30 bites, named 'experiences', that lasts for four hours, featuring crunchy fish bones with lemon, garlic and cayenne, bone marrow on toast with horseradish ash, served with edible cutlery or clay-covered potatoes refashioned as pebbles. To fully enjoy the experience, the staff has studied with actors and psychologists to create a completely interactive and immersive culinary show, including playing games, or being invited into the kitchen to bite into a blood and foie gras macaron.

— 54 —
LIDO 84

Gardone Riviera
Corso Zanardelli, 196, 25083 Gardone Riviera (BS)

◆ TO VISIT BEFORE YOU DIE BECAUSE

You will be blown away by chef Camanini's 'cacio e pepe' pasta boiled inside a pig's bladder while marvelling at the blue tones of Lake Garda.

Just six months after Lido 84 was opened by Riccardo Camanini and his brother Giancarlo in 2014, they were awarded a Michelin star. Today it is one of the most well-respected restaurants in Italy. The restaurant, which used to be an outdoor swimming pool, sits right on Lake Garda's shoreline, in the town of Gardone Riviera, with incredible views of the water and the old castle of La Rocca di Manerba. In the dining room, which is a homage to 1960s Art Deco and the colours of the surrounding nature, chef Riccardo Camanini is one of Italy's most promising talents, using innovative cooking methods to bring out the natural flavours of the local produce. Highlights on the menu include the surreal version of 'cacio e pepe' pasta boiled inside a pig's bladder, which is then theatrically sliced open at the table.

www.ristorantelido84.com

— 55 —
VILLA FELTRINELLI

ITALY

Gargnano
Via Rimembranza 38–40, Gargnano 25084

MODERN
ITALIAN

◆ TO VISIT BEFORE YOU DIE BECAUSE

It is a treat to relax in the afternoon next to the swimming pool, where home-made ice creams are served and then enjoy the evening while breeze sipping a strawberry martini in front of the peaceful lake.

Villa Feltrinelli is a villa built on the western bank of Lake Garda in 1892 by the Feltrinelli family. They first commissioned it to serve as a retreat, providing an escape from the heat of the summer in Milan. In 1997, Bob Burns, a celebrated hotelier, transformed it into a luxury hotel. Inside the neo-Gothic design with fine wood panelling, wood-inlay ceilings, stained-glass windows and delicate frescoes, the Michelin-starred chef, Stefano Baiocco, creates exquisite dishes with fresh and local ingredients from the restaurant's kitchen garden, making unique and creative combinations with the herbs and ingredients.

www.villafeltrinelli.com

— 56 —
ELKANO

SPAIN

Getaria

Herrerieta Kalea 2, 20808 Getaria

TRADITIONAL
BASQUE

◆ TO VISIT BEFORE YOU DIE BECAUSE

The best time to visit Elkano is in April or May when wild Atlantic turbot is at the peak of its season, and you can hear chef Aitor Arregui's passionating stories about the fishing season and the work they do with the local fishermen.

In Getaria, a small fishing village on the Bay of Biscay 15 miles west of San Sebastián, there is a most acclaimed family restaurant, named Elkano. 'Seasonal', 'head-to-tail' and 'sustainable' are used by all chefs today, but at Elkano these words just describe the way cooking has been done there since Pedro Arregui opened the restaurant in 1964. Today, on the parrillas outside, you can still see whole fishes, caught by the local fishermen, grilling. The highlight of the menu is a whole turbot, cooked on the charcoal grill and served on the bone, with the soft and tender flesh around the throat area, called the cheeks (kokotxas in Basque), being particularly good. This is a favourite with the locals and is served in different ways. Al pil pil is the most traditional method of preparation, served with pil pil sauce made from olive oil, garlic and small local chillies. Those delicacies are more than a souvenir of the culture and traditions of Getaria, they represent the whole Arregui family history.

150 RESTAURANTS YOU NEED TO VISIT BEFORE YOU DIE

CHAMBRE SÉPARÉE

BELGIUM	**Ghent** Keizer Karelstraat 1, 9000 Ghent	CHEF'S COUNTER / OPEN FIRE

◆ TO VISIT BEFORE YOU DIE BECAUSE

Chef Kobe Desramaults's unique way of cooking lobster, in the high heat of the oven and then dipped in ice cubes so the flesh remains soft inside, is a must-try.

Kobe Desramaults, the chef of the former renowned restaurant In de Wulf in the Belgian countryside, has opened his new place in the city of Ghent, Chambre Séparée. He has come back to what he loves the most: cooking pure and natural products using different forms of fire in front of the guests, to provide a unique dining experience. Inspired by the sushi counters in Japan, he designed a place where the customer directly accesses the open kitchen, watching the theatre play and accompanying the chef through his performance. The restaurant serves one tasting menu consisting of 20 courses, for which the dishes are prepared according to the seasons and with whatever ingredients the farmers supply. The must-tries are the North Sea lobster, with its claw served nearly raw and its head pressed in a duck press, and the Steenvoorde pigeon matured for six weeks, with fermented tea and roasted hay, which you eat with your fingers!

— 58 —
EL CELLER DE CAN ROCA

SPAIN

Girona
Can Sunyer 48, 17007, Girona

MODERN
SPANISH

◆ TO VISIT BEFORE YOU DIE BECAUSE

You will be invited to visit Josep Roca's magical walk-in cellar, where he has re-created the physical sensations inspired by each of his favourite wines, to run your fingers through ball bearings to express champagne, caress the velvet of great burgundy and ripple the green-gold silk of Riesling.

El Celler de Can Roca is located in the medieval city of Girona in Catalonia. The three Roca brothers who own and run the restaurant bring complementary skills to the creative process: Joan as a chef, Josep as a sommelier and Jordi as a pâtissier. Arriving through a secluded garden, diners enter the glass-panelled maze of a dining room that encircles a courtyard. The restaurant has received a lot of attention for its amuse-bouche presentations, such as the bonsai tree where caramelised olives stuffed with anchovies hang from the branches, and a paper lantern that features five small bites, each representing a different country: Korea, Peru, China, Mexico and Morocco. Combining modern techniques with a dose of fantasy, the food is quite complex, designed to evoke memories, emotions and the landscape of the region with an emphasis on aromas:

from smoking the vegetables, caramelising the meats and crisping the fishes. The menu may feature a crunchy bonbon of pigeon with sherry, an Iberian suckling pig blanquette with Riesling and black garlic, or a salt cod brandade with olive oil, celery and shallots. Jordi Roca's masterful desserts, such as the mint, apple and cucumber granita, create a beautiful transition from the savoury to the sweet part of the menu.

www.cellercanroca.com

— 59 —
HENNE KIRKEBY KRO

	Henne	
DENMARK	Strandvejen 234, 6854 Henne	**FARM-TO-TABLE**

◆ TO VISIT BEFORE YOU DIE BECAUSE

You could spend a night or two while exploring the Danish countryside to discover the exceptional British chef's cuisine.

Located in a small, picturesque village in Denmark, Henne Kirkeby Kro is surrounded by beautiful countryside, a sprawling garden with vegetables, berry bushes and flowers, and the nearby Wadden Sea. In the intimate atmosphere and charm of this former royal staging post, Paul Cunningham, a British-born chef who has worked in many of Denmark's finest kitchens, cooks solely with nature's freshest ingredients. The result is a cuisine anchored by Danish ingredients wrapped in French and English tradition and combined with his own innovation: he pairs an Indian spice such as vadouvan with a Danish crustacean, a lobster Thermidor or steak au poivre without a single twist.

DENMARK	**Holte** Søllerødvej 35, 2840 Holte	TRADITIONAL FRENCH

◆ TO VISIT BEFORE YOU DIE BECAUSE
This is the place to taste unforgettable desserts that are real artistic culinary creations.

Located in idyllic surroundings with the village pond in front and the woods behind, Søllerød Kro is a one-star Michelin restaurant set in a seventeenth-century thatched-roof inn, situated a 25-minute drive from Copenhagen. Inside the elegant and classic dining room, chef Brian Mark Hansen and restaurant manager Jan Restorff welcome you warmly, and present you with delicious tastes in terms of both wine and food, so that you experience a meal filled with happiness, exploration and surprise. The cuisine mostly combines solid classic French techniques with Scandinavian seasonal ingredients. The breathtakingly balanced flavours and textures are paired with fabulous wine from one of the best wine lists in Scandinavia. Suited waiters with silver trays serve you scallops from Norway surrounded by dehydrated Jerusalem artichokes, hazelnuts and a brown butter foam, and roasted foie gras with beets and an elderberry jus. The colours and designs of the desserts are exceptional: 'The Snow Queen's Tale' with coconut, passion fruit and vanilla; 'The Well-insulated Green Fantasy' with pistachio, thyme and hay milk; and 'The Brown Finale' with chocolate, walnuts and arabica are real pieces of art.

— 61 —
MIKLA

TURKEY

Istanbul
The Marmara Pera, Meşrutiyet Caddesi 15,
34430 Beyoğlu, Istanbul

MODERN TURKISH

◆ TO VISIT BEFORE YOU DIE BECAUSE

You will taste the chef's version of Balik Ekmek, the traditional fish sandwich, in front of the unmissable 360-degree views of Istanbul with the Bosphorus reflecting the city lights.

From the eighteenth-floor rooftop terrace of the Marmara Pera hotel, Mikla has one of the best views of Istanbul. The restaurant itself is sophisticated, with sleek minimalist styling, retro flourishes and cosy lighting. In the glass kitchen, the Finnish-Swedish chef, Mehmet Gürs, who was born and raised in Scandinavia and then trained in the USA, draws upon his wide range of influences to cook his creations. Gürs has developed a new Anatolian cuisine that rediscovers a culinary heritage that is in danger of disappearing, by supporting independent farmers and producers, and exploring ancient cooking techniques to keep traditions alive. Throughout the year, Gürs travels widely across Turkey with fabulous food anthropologist Tangör Tan to meet artisan growers and producers, and to source rare ingredients such as halhali olives and halwa from smaller villages all over the country. The chef's elegant simplicity from his Scandinavian heritage is shown in a delicate version of manti, a Turkish filled pasta served with yoghurt home-made from raw milk, slow-cooked lamb with plums and aubergines, and pumpkin and saffron ice cream with apple molasses.

www.miklarestaurant.com

TURKEY	**Istanbul** SALT Galata, Bankalar Avenue, 34420 Karaköy, Istanbul	MODERN TURKISH

◆ TO VISIT BEFORE YOU DIE BECAUSE

You might see chef Maksut Aşkar and his mum giggling while they are cooking his modern version of the içli köfte in the kitchen.

Located in the cultural institution and exhibition space Salt Galata, in the former Ottoman Bank, Neolokal has stunning views of the Golden Horn in Istanbul. Chef Maksut Aşkar is a member of Gastronomika, Turkey's Slow Food movement, and believes it is possible to save organic and socially responsible eating habits in Istanbul. To do so, he showcases local and seasonal ingredients in dishes that explore and redefine traditional Anatolian cuisine, following its history, culture and tradition. His philosophy goes back to the roots,

focusing on the idea of community spirit and collectivity, using ingredients from a farm located 20 kilometres outside the city and growing his own herbs in a miniature garden on the top-floor terrace. The highlights on the menu are lamb mutancana – slow-cooked leg of lamb with dried fruits, freekeh wheat, za'tar and grilled lettuce – and octopus scented with lavender and served with lemony potato cream, lemon zest and orange powder.

— 63 —
SOHO HOUSE, MANDOLIN TERRACE

TURKEY

Istanbul
Evliya Çelebi Mahallesi,
34430 Beyoğlu, Istanbul

MODERN INTERNATIONAL

◆ TO VISIT BEFORE YOU DIE BECAUSE

The terrace is the ideal place to see spectacular sunsets over the waters of Istanbul's Golden Horn and Old Town, while drinking a glass of wine and watching the local crowd.

In Istanbul, the private club Soho House is housed in a sumptuous renovated nineteenth-century mansion, built for a Genoese merchant before serving as the US embassy and consulate general for most of the twentieth century. Spread over three floors, the grandeur of the place is an experience in itself: there are masterful frescoes on the ceilings, while extravagant Carrara marble and precious woods signal the decorum of this historic and yet very contemporary mansion. Some of the vast spaces have been given playful new roles: there is a Powder Room of epic proportions; the grand balcony under the entablature is now a huge smoking terrace; and the new bar on the second floor stretches across the entire depth of the building. The much-loved poached egg on avocado toast remains a winner, but if you are looking for a more local flavour, give the menemen (traditional Turkish scrambled eggs with peppers and feta) a go.

www.sohohouseistanbul.com

SWEDEN	**Järpen** Fäviken Magasinet, Fäviken 216, 83794 Järpen	MODERN SCANDINAVIAN

◆ TO VISIT BEFORE YOU DIE BECAUSE

Fäviken offers one of the most exclusive and isolated culinary experiences, which has become bucket-list material for food obsessives.

Located near the Åre ski resort in Jämtland, more than 600 kilometres north of Stockholm, Fäviken is often billed as the world's most isolated restaurant. In the picturesque 12-seat dining room, with pork belly and trout hanging on the walls, all guests are served simultaneously by the head chef, Magnus Nilsson. Being a harvester, hunter and preserver, at least 70 per cent of everything that is served in Nilsson's restaurant comes from the more than 8,000-acre property and the remaining ingredients are sourced from local villages. The tasting menu changes according to the season and the availability of ingredients. Dishes include raw cow's heart with bone marrow, served with grey pea flowers on a toast, and wild trout roe in dried pig's blood. The giant scallop arrives in its shell floating in a bath, steaming over burning juniper branches.

— 65 —
HIŠA FRANKO

SLOVENIA

Kobarid
Hiša Franko d.o.o., Staro selo 1,
5222 Kobarid

**MODERN
SLOVENIAN**

◆ TO VISIT BEFORE YOU DIE BECAUSE

You can sleep over in Hiša Franko at the 10-room mansion and wake up in front of the mountains, next to crystal-clear rivers, and discover Slovenia's still unknown region.

In the western Slovenian countryside with views of green fields and soaring mountains, Hiša Franko is a home steeped in history. Built in 1868, it is purported to be where Ernest Hemingway wrote *A Farewell to Arms*. This is the place where the entirely self-taught chef Ana Ros, deeply rooted in her Alpine region, forages apples, chestnuts, and mushrooms from the surroundings while she is collecting berries, cheese and mushrooms from local farmers. She ferments the seasonal riches herself and inserts them into her personal seasonally changing menus. You might try the sour cream and anchovy mousse with smoked beef marrow, salty lollipops of crusted cheese set in moss-covered wood logs, and raviolis stuffed with Bovski sir sheep's cheese, bought from the local mountain farmers and kept in a temperature-controlled cellar alongside the wines her husband, Valter, selects.

www.hisafranko.com

FRANCE	La Madelaine-Sous-Montreuil	MODERN
	19 Rue de la Grenouillère, 62170	FRENCH
	La Madelaine-sous-Montreuil	

◆ TO VISIT BEFORE YOU DIE BECAUSE

Chef Alexandre Gauthier describes himself as a contemporary author in the kitchen, constantly reinventing each one of his recipes.

In the northern Pas-de-Calais region, inside his family's countryside mansion, chef Alexandre Gauthier built a splendid glass-paned futurist extension surrounded by nature, where he reveals flavours like an alchemist. Gauthier is inspired by modern art, circus and theatre, performing off the beaten track, and relishing the purity of ingredients. He expresses himself in a personal, unbridled cuisine in which the freshness and wildness of produce sing the praises of the seasons. Showing his creativity and sincerity, his fabulous dishes include a large grilled oyster with an arugula pistou and a foam of seaside, exquisite honey taken from the hive in the garden, which you chew until only one wax ball remains in your mouth, and a mantilla of chocolate placed on a cream of almonds, on which three drops of crystal vinegar have been dropped delicately from a pipette.

— 67 —
AZURMENDI

Larrabetzu
Barrio Legina s/n, (48195) Larrabetzu (Bizkaia)

◆ TO VISIT BEFORE YOU DIE BECAUSE

This environmentally friendly restaurant recycles its own waste, as well as harvesting rainfall and cooling itself using geothermal energy.

Perched on a hillside, Azurmendi tells the story of the Basque Country's finest produce through an all-encompassing culinary experience. With sustainability and technique as key concepts in his kitchen, chef Eneko Atxa has cultivated strong relationships with nearby growers and suppliers. He leads guests on a journey, starting in the interior garden where a picnic with different snacks is served.

Subsequently, they are welcomed to the kitchen for another selection of snacks and then they go through to a new greenhouse space to taste seasonal products like fermented apple juice, herbs and kaipiritxa. Diners will enjoy, for example, truffled eggs cooked 'from the inside out' with part of the yolk removed and replaced with truffle consommé, and the tear peas, purple onion gel and corn bread signature dishes.

azurmendi.restaurant

— 68 —
KOKS

**DENMARK
(FAROE ISLANDS)**

Leynavatn
Frammi við Gjónna, Leynavatn,
Faroe Islands

**MODERN
SCANDINAVIAN**

◆ TO VISIT BEFORE YOU DIE BECAUSE

Here you can discover the natural paradise of the Faroe Islands and experience the freshest salmon, mussels and langoustines on earth.

The Faroe Islands, 18 tiny islands located between Iceland and Norway, are probably one of Europe's best-kept secrets. With the unique local culinary tradition and amazing terroir, Koks is a fine-dining restaurant that explores and experiments with the surrounding landscape of sea, fjords, fields and meadows. In the 23-seat gourmet restaurant with its breathtaking panoramic views over the sea, the decor features wooden floorboards, lambskins on the chairs and oak tables free of tablecloths or folded napkins. Chef Poul Ziska is one of the chief proponents of representing Scandinavia's New Nordic movement with elegance, freshness and simplicity. He creates dishes rooted in local traditions using ingredients he finds on the rocky shores down below his dining room and traditional products such as 'restkød', 'garnatálg' and 'skerpikjøt'. The menu comprises 19 unforgettably delicate courses, including such dishes as raw Mahogany clam, sliced over a kale purée, ocean quahogs garnished with dried elderflower, or raw clams with elderflower.

L'AIR DU TEMPS

BELGIUM

Liernu
Rue de la Croix Monet 2,
5310 Liernu

FARM-TO-TABLE/
MODERN EUROPEAN

◆ TO VISIT BEFORE YOU DIE BECAUSE

Here you can experience the chef's connection to nature, and its importance in his concept of cooking in the luminous dining room overlooking the garden.

Born in South Korea and adopted by a Belgian family at five years of age, Sang-Hoon Degeimbre is the chef of L'Air du Temps in Belgium. Self taught, he spent ten years working as a sommelier in world-renowned Belgian restaurants, before opening his own. Today, in a restored farmhouse nestled in the slopes of the Wallonian countryside, Degeimbre has just reopened the newly refurbished restaurant in a completely new space, where the dining room overlooks the garden, emphasising his connection to nature and its importance to his cooking. Degeimbre has created his own identity based on local products, and vegetables, herbs and aromatic plants from his two-hectare garden. He is highly sensitive to waste and sustainability and is also keen to use modern technologies to find the best possible techniques for achieving maximum flavour, such as ultrasound to filter molecules found within ingredients to produce delicate perfumed waters. At L'Air du Temps, guests enjoy original and tasty recipes, such as his signature dish 'Liernu' made completely of vegetables, which evolves with the seasons: with many flowers in the spring, more roots in the autumn and lacto-fermented vegetables during the winter.

PORTUGAL	Lisbon Largo de Sao Carlos, 10 Chiado, Lisbon 1200-410	MODERN EUROPEAN

◆ TO VISIT BEFORE YOU DIE BECAUSE

For foodies, it is thoroughly fulfilling to understand chef José Avillez artistic mind through the poetry and the harmony of his dishes.

José Avillez is the first Portuguese chef to earn two Michelin stars. He stands out thanks to his endless creativity, with each one of his restaurants offering a completely different culinary experience. In Lisbon's Chaido district, Belcanto is the intimate fine-dining establishment he designed with leather seats and art installations.
He expresses the romance of Portugal through his tasting menu, starting with a pig served with an edible packet of thinly fried potatoes, an orange sauce with black garlic, and a marinated and braised mackerel with pickled vegetable confetti and pinhão. As main courses, the chef revives classics such as the 'Golden Eggs', cooked at 62°C for 45 minutes, served with crispy bread and glistening wild mushrooms, and the 'Dip in the Sea', a sea bass with seaweed and bivalves.

THE ARAKI

UNITED KINGDOM	London 12 New Burlington Street, London W1S 3BH	JAPANESE OMAKASE

◆ TO VISIT BEFORE YOU DIE BECAUSE

It is wonderful to be able to sit at the counter and experience an exclusive omakase sushi meal, like in Japan, but in the heart of London.

Japanese sushi master Mitsuhiro Araki – one of just a handful of sushi chefs to be awarded three Michelin stars – left Tokyo to open up The Araki in London, with just nine covers. The design of this intimate place is subtle and serene with a focus on the cypress wood counter where the chef delicately presents each part of his omakase chef's menu. As in the most traditional sushi counters in Japan, the rice bites are served with the instruction to eat them with the fingers, fish-side down to maximise the flavour. Araki adapted his traditional edomae sushi to incorporate European produce, serving salmon sushi (practically unheard of in Japan) and luxury ingredients such as caviar and truffles. He reaches the apogee of the meal with his signature tuna sourced from Spain and Ireland, following a set sequence: first the akami (red meat), then the chotoro and last the rich otoro that melts softly on the tongue.

the-araki.com

BUBBLEDOGS
KITCHEN TABLE

UNITED KINGDOM	London	CHEF'S COUNTER
	70 Charlotte Street, London W1T 4QG	

◆ TO VISIT BEFORE YOU DIE BECAUSE

You will discover a fine-dining counter hidden at the back of a hot dog joint.

Bubbledogs Kitchen Table is a tiny, modern-European restaurant, hidden behind a curtain at the back of champagne and hot dog joint Bubbledogs. Chef James Knappett, who has worked at The Ledbury (London) and Per Se (New York), shakes the pans and takes centre stage of the U-shaped open kitchen and counter that seats just 19 people. Right in front of the diners, the chef and his team flaunt their culinary skills as they prepare the 14-course menu, which changes daily and incorporates only the freshest produce. Knappett's cuisine is inspired by contemporary European cooking with a strong focus on British traditions and ingredients that are described on the menu by just a single word: 'beetroot' is an earthy blend of beetroot, fennel and garlic scapes, while 'chicken' is a combination of chicken skin and grilled onion with burrata milk.

— 73 —
CHILTERN FIREHOUSE

UNITED KINGDOM

London
1 Chiltern Street, Marylebone, London W1U 7PA

MODERN INTERNATIONAL

◆ TO VISIT BEFORE YOU DIE BECAUSE
Kate Moss and Cara Delevigne are regulars of this fashionable place.

Led by the famous chef Nuno Mendes, the restaurant has lit up the Marylebone food scene since its opening. Decked out like a brassy and lowly lit New York basement bar, Chiltern Firehouse feels every bit as buzzy as its reputation suggests, drawing a starry crowd and impressing with its lively atmosphere and top-notch food in a beautiful red-brick building. Dishes are cosmopolitan, such as the souped-up versions of eggs Benedict, buttermilk pancakes and French toast on the breakfast menu. As for lunch, there is a newfangled Caesar salad with strips of crispy chicken skin; savoury crab doughnuts with coral dust; buttermilk-fried chicken and monkfish cooked over pine and short rib of beef. Its discreet courtyard entrance and hidden smoking lounge merely add to the restaurant's mystique and sophistication.

— 74 —
HEDONE

UNITED
KINGDOM

London

301–303 Chiswick High Road, London W4 4HH

MODERN
ENGLISH

◆ TO VISIT BEFORE YOU DIE BECAUSE
Chef Mikael Jonsson's sourdough bread, considered by many as the best in the capital, is a must-try.

Restaurant Hedone is a Michelin-starred restaurant situated in Chiswick, just outside London. Swedish-born chef and owner Mikael Jonsson was a trained chef who then became a lawyer. His passion for food and being an ingredient expert first led him to become a food blogger, before he rediscovered his gastronomic side and opening Hedone. At first he had no other idea than to offer people good food in a relaxed environment where they could feel at home, and, prior to opening Hedone, he had never worked in a professional kitchen. Yet, after being open for only 14 months, Hedone was awarded its Michelin star. The food stands out thanks to Jonsson's extensive knowledge and sourcing of the finest ingredients. His fresh produce comes from Paris, Scotland and the south coast of England and the menu evolves according to what arrives. Highlights of the menu include smoked haddock tart and foie gras in a sourdough crisp and seaweed on savoury custard, followed by French white asparagus with tarragon hollandaise.

— 75 —
THE LEDBURY

UNITED
KINGDOM

London
127 Ledbury Road, Notting Hill,
London W11 2AQ

MODERN
BRITISH

◆ TO VISIT BEFORE YOU DIE BECAUSE

It is an experience to see chef Brett Graham's refined and elegant way of plating, on mottled stones and textured ceramics.

Located in the private and fashionable neighbourhood of Notting Hill, The Ledbury has an elegant, dark-grey exterior. Inside, on the well-spaced white-clothed tables, waiters serve the dishes inspired by Australian-born chef Brett Graham's background. Graham's style of food is one of complex flavours, merging French technique with British and Japanese ingredients. He is passionate about reducing food waste, encouraging his team to use the whole animal and produce otherwise thrown away by farmers, such as white beetroot. The chef sources British ingredients from his vast network of small-scale suppliers, in order to serve the best of the country's land and sea with a great eclecticism and appreciation of fabulous produce. He is also a keen hunter. Some of Graham's most iconic dishes include flame-grilled mackerel with pickled cucumber, Celtic mustard and shiso, and a tartare of sea bream topped with oyster chantilly and green beans, paired with green almonds, apricot and slices of foie gras.

www.theledbury.com

| UNITED KINGDOM | London 56 Shoreditch High Street, London E1 6JJ | MODERN BRITISH |

◆ TO VISIT BEFORE YOU DIE BECAUSE

James Lowe is one of the hottest British chefs, and has a great sense of detail and taste.

Lyle's is housed in trendy Shoreditch's Tea Building in an industrial setting with white walls, high ceilings and wooden designer furniture, with sunlight streaming in through the original warehouse windows. Talented chef James Lowe first worked as a pilot, until he changed his mind and began his culinary experience at Heston Blumenthal, St John and The River Café, before opening his own restaurant. Lowe pays great attention to detail and believes working with producers is key: fish is couriered from Cornwall daily while every week in summer the Lyle's team drives to the south coast to pick fruit and vegetables. Throughout his à la carte lunch menu and dinner set menu, the food is as unpretentiously brilliant as the young chef. Expect the best of local produce and technical precision at its best: slightly smoked eel and horseradish, structured cabbage with plump mussels and seaweed, and generous blood cake with chicory and burnt apple. The thick asparagus, grilled and sprinkled with walnuts and Spenwood cheese, and the treacle tart with raw milk ice cream are not to be missed.

SKETCH

	London	
UNITED KINGDOM	9 Conduit Street, London W1S 2XG	**MODERN INTERNATIONAL**

◆ TO VISIT BEFORE YOU DIE BECAUSE

At Sketch, an 'Alice in Wonderland' teatime awaits you in artist David Shrigley's curious gallery.

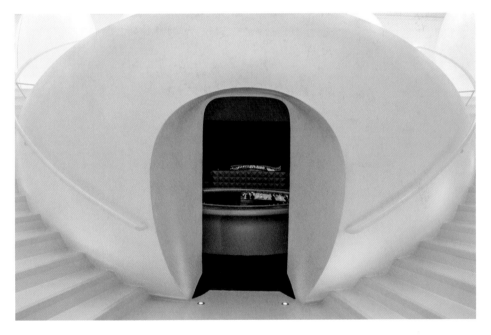

In the heart of London's chic Mayfair, Sketch houses an art gallery and several hip restaurants and bars under its roof. The dining room is one of the most playful and pinkest places, attracting a stylish crowd and serving chef Pierre Gagnaire's award-winning menu. The walls, with 200 original prints and drawings by Turner Prize-winning David Shrigley, add a real sense of fun to the place. In the Michelin-starred restaurant, the 'caviar man' in a panama hat and pale blazer serves the guests a spoonful of Russian sturgeon roe alongside 'Egg', made of Comté cheese and quail egg cooked at 63°C, and 'Soldiers', made of cheesy toast strips. If you visit for afternoon tea you are likely to meet the fashion crowd, and at night you can sip cocktails when Sketch turns into a bar. And do not forget to check out the cool cocoon-like toilets.

UNITED KINGDOM	London	CHEF'S COUNTER
	41 Redchurch Street, London E2 7DJ	

◆ TO VISIT BEFORE YOU DIE BECAUSE

You will have a personal experience with the chef Nuno Mendes, the Portuguese pioneer cook in London, at his small counter.

Before being a serial restaurateur, Nuno Mendes founded the cult pop-up known as the Loft Project, whereby some of the world's finest experimental chefs would prepare food in their own home and guests would dine communally around the kitchen table, in a uniquely intimate environment. In London he opened a 14-seater 'secret' 'kitchen, table and wine room', called Mãos (meaning 'hands' in Portuguese), above the high-end clothes shop Hostem in Shoreditch, to provide a fine-dining experience for the guests. Strongly influenced by both Iberian and Japanese cultures, Mendes' food can be as subversive as it is imaginative, recontextualising traditional ingredients and techniques into a masterpiece of flavours. Dishes could include anything from smoked Kobe beef with sweet peas and ramsons to wild turbot with seaweed sofrito and magnolia leaf, and mushroom and kombu chawanmushi.

bluemountain.school/maos

— 79 —
IKOYI

UNITED KINGDOM	London	MODERN AFRICAN
	1 St. James's Market, London, SW1Y 4AH	

◆ TO VISIT BEFORE YOU DIE BECAUSE

At Ikoyi you will experience the very first West African fine-dining establishment to earn a Michelin star in London.

Right off Piccadilly Circus in the centre of London, Ikoyi was named after an affluent district of Lagos. This is the place where chef Jeremy Chan and his business partner, Iré Hassan-Odukale, chose to introduce West African ingredients, flavours and references into the realm of fine dining. They created their innovative cuisine based upon the interpretation of mostly unknown ingredients in Europe, such as Grains of Selim and *ndolé* leaves, in order to invigorate typical British dishes, such as Orkney scallops or wild, Scottish turbot. With the colourful plates combining bold heat and umami, guests will experience plantains festooned with vividly cerise, dehydrated raspberry powder and a *dambu nama*, a dried-beef floss set atop a delicate tartlet of whipped bone-marrow pancake and Sun Sweet melon from Mantua, dressed with a crayfish salt, cured beetroot and a fresh walnut oil.

ikoyilondon.com

— 80 —
XU

UNITED
KINGDOM

London
30 Rupert Street, London W1D 6DL

MODERN
TAIWANESE

◆ TO VISIT BEFORE YOU DIE BECAUSE

You will feel adventurously transported onto a train, in a first-class carriage in the 1930s in Taipei.

In the heart of Chinatown on Rupert Street, Xu is an imaginative reinterpretation of 1930s Taipei inspired by old Chinese movies and theatre. The restaurant concept pays homage to the rich history and cultural past of Taiwan, creating a magical atmosphere in a pink and green palette, with railway clocks and wooden furniture. On the tables of the elegant booths in the dining room, the extremely savoury Taiwanese food that is served ranges from the peanut lotus crisps with peanut, chilli and winter-melon syrup and the crispy pan-fried soup dumplings to char siu Iberico pork with braised cucumber and sesame, mixing a Cantonese barbecue dish with top-notch European produce. Xu also prides itself on its selection of Taiwanese teas, which it sources directly from Taiwan.

— 81 —
DIVERXO

Madrid

SPAIN NH Eurobuilding, Calle de Padre Damián 23, 28036 Madrid **FUSION**

◆ TO VISIT BEFORE YOU DIE BECAUSE

You will have a surprising Spanish-Asian arty performance in a wittily decorated room.

To book one of the 30 seats at DiverXO, the hottest restaurant in Madrid, is not without challenges. With reservations only taken up to 30 days in advance, you will have to be quick, or lucky enough to grab a cancellation.The reason is the surprising Spanish-Asian fusion cuisine of chef David Muñoz. The young chef perfected his oriental kitchen techniques while working at Nobu and Hakkasan in London, which is why hearty Iberian ingredients are combined with the flavours of China and Japan. European classics such as cochinillo (suckling pig) are given Eastern touches, and steamed carrot dim sum is served with bull tail noodle soup. Like a real performance set in a dining room whose walls are wittily decorated with winged pigs, the waiters serve the culinary creations on smooth, white ceramic plates, as if they were putting paint on a canvas. The presentation of the dishes changes regularly, following the chef's inspiration: one day, the gleamingly fresh monkfish is teamed with 'potato glass', which is in fact multicoloured shards of potato, while the next day it is scattered with seeds and sauces like a Jackson Pollock painting.

diverxo.com

— 82 —
DANIEL BERLIN

SWEDEN

Malmö
Diligensvägen 21,
273 92 Skåne-Tranås, Malmö

**MODERN
SCANDINAVIAN**

◆ TO VISIT BEFORE YOU DIE BECAUSE

The culinary experience is set in a very intimate dining room in the most charming Swedish countryside cottage.

Daniel Berlin's restaurant sits at the southern tip of Sweden in the small town of Skåne-Tranås, housed in a tiny cottage an hour north of Malmö. Berlin has made his name by crafting perfectly plated dishes, and serving local food that he grows, forages and hunts for himself in the surrounding countryside and coastline. At least 80 per cent of the kitchen's produce is harvested from his own three-acre plot during the summer, with the rest grown or foraged within three miles of the restaurant. Drinks and amuse-bouches served in the garden during the summer are perfectly matched with French wines and refreshing juices. In the tiny 14-seat dining room, the chef often emerges from the kitchen to serve and explain a tranche of lightly smoked mackerel with cucumber, cauliflower, brown butter and wild herbs, or yeast pancake with pork fat and caraway, or a hackberry flower dish paired with raspberry, rhubarb, juniper and spruce shoots.

www.danielberlin.se

147

DAL PESCATORE

ITALY

Mantova

Riserva del Parco – Canneto S/O, I-46013,
Canneto S/O, Mantova, Lombardia

TRADITIONAL
ITALIAN

◆ TO VISIT BEFORE YOU DIE BECAUSE

Dal Pescatore is an iconic temple of Italian gastronomic history, and chef Nadia Santini's tortelli di zucca are a must.

Located in a bucolic countryside setting in the Parco dell'Oglio in northern Italy, not far from the beautiful city of Mantua, Dal Pescatore offers the combination of a restaurant, and a hymn to good taste and family values. The success is due to the owners, the Santini family, who have been at the helm here for generations. Owner and restaurant manager Antonio Santini's grandparents opened the place in 1925, and Nadia, Antonio's wife, was trained by her husband's grandmother Teresa, when she married into the family in the 1970s. She has held three Michelin stars at the restaurant since 1996 and still runs the kitchen today with her son Giovanni. In the dining room, Antonio circulates and talks with guests, while Alberto carefully decants a Barolo wine. The cuisine is classic Italian, with vegetables and herbs grown on the property. From the enormous decorated menu with a cover that changes seasonally, do not miss the grilled eel and the legendary rich pumpkin tortelli (Tortelli di zucca) with their amaretti-crumb filling, rolled in soft egg-yellow pasta.

FLOCONS DE SEL

FRANCE

Megève
1775 Route du Leutaz,
74120 Megève

MODERN
FRENCH

◆ TO VISIT BEFORE YOU DIE BECAUSE

You will experience the elegance of a luxurious Alpine chalet, while savouring amuse-bouches in the middle of the mountains.

Situated in Megève, in the heart of Haute-Savoie, Flocons de Sel can be found in a charming chalet with pine-panelled walls, wood-burning stoves and cathedral-like ceilings with beautiful mountain views. Chef Emmanuel Renaut trained in Paris at Le Crillon and at Claridge's in London for several years, before returning to France to open his own restaurant and be awarded three Michelin stars. To create the subtle and inventive cuisine, the staff go out foraging twice a day to source produce and ingredients from nature and suppliers up to 100 kilometres from the restaurant, presenting diners with ultra-elegant juniper beignets, and the legendary Noires de Crimée tomatoes with marigold under a thin ice disc made from tomato skins, and a selection of wild mushrooms, lemon balm jelly, chives and iced wood sorrel.

— 85 —
MIRAZUR

FRANCE

Menton
30 Avenue Aristide Briand, 06500 Menton

MODERN FRENCH

This is where you can discover the richness of chef Mauro Colagreco's boldly contrasting flavours, while enjoying views of the Mediterranean landscape.

High atop the cliffs of Menton, Mirazur is an idyllic spot in which to gaze at spectacular views of the French Riviera. In the kitchen, three Michelin star chef Mauro Colagreco, who trained under chefs Alain Passard, Alain Ducasse, Guy Martin and Bernard Loiseau, takes inspiration from his Argentinian-Italian heritage and the local French region to create his refined and sensitive cuisine, which is one of the best in the world. Colagreco juggles prawns and squid from Italy, fish from the Menton coast, and flowers, fruits and vegetables that are gathered each morning from his own garden to create the daily menu. Diners can expect a feast of sparklingly fresh seafood such as oysters with tapioca, shallot cream and pear, or beetroot cooked in salt crust, served with an Ossetra caviar sauce.

— 86 —
IL LUOGO DI
AIMO E NADIA

ITALY

Milan
Via Privata Raimondo
Montecuccoli, 6, 20147 Milan

**TRADITIONAL
ITALIAN**

◆ TO VISIT BEFORE YOU DIE BECAUSE

The legendary spaghettone col cipollotto, created by chef Aimo Moroni in
1965, is still on the menu.

Within a fresh, white interior with contemporary art pieces and sculpture, Il Luogo di Aimo e Nadia is the legendary two-Michelin-starred restaurant in Milan founded by chef Aimo Moroni and his wife Nadia, which has been owned by the same family for over 50 years. The restaurant is now led by two young chefs, Alessandro Negrini and Fabio Pisani, from the mountains of Lombardy and the southern region of Puglia respectively, who have built relationships with producers and farmers all over Italy, just like Aimo did. At Il Luogo di Aimo e Nadia, diners will taste Italian cuisine at its finest: the uncomplicated and unpretentious ingredients are mastered by the concepts of taste, and the pursuit of the best products available. One of the highlights is the signature dish invented by Aimo Moroni more than 50 years ago: the spaghettone col cipollotto, made of semolina and durum wheat pasta cooked with green onions, hot pepper sauce, olive oil and basil.

ITALY

Milan

Via Giorgio Vasari 1,
(angolo Via L. Muratori), 20135 Milan

**TRADITIONAL
ITALIAN**

◆ TO VISIT BEFORE YOU DIE BECAUSE

Trippa is a new style of trattoria, with soul food made by Diego Rossi, a young and talented chef.

Trippa is a new style of trattoria, which focuses on traditional dishes with a twist, that was created by a lover of gastronomy, Pietro Caroli, and the young talented chef Diego Rossi. Rossi, who has worked in several Michelin-starred restaurants, translates his great skills into home-cooked seasonal food with the highest quality ingredients, which he sources directly from the producers. Everyone would like to experience his Italian cuisine because it is created with love and brings a smile to the face. From the dining room, guests can watch Rossi frying tripe, plating his vitello tonnato Milanese and cooking the airy white sauce of his sumptuous lasagne, all on the short daily menu. Trippa's laid-back casual atmosphere and friendly team make it an amazing place to eat and feel at home. And as soon as you put his dishes in your mouth, you understand Italian food has been brought to another level.

www.trippamilano.it

— 88 —
OSTERIA FRANCESCANA

ITALY	**Modena** Via Stella 22, 41121 Modena	MODERN ITALIAN

◆ TO VISIT BEFORE YOU DIE BECAUSE

It is said to be the best restaurant in the world, and experiencing chef Massimo Bottura's storytelling dinner is a must.

Osteria Francescana, which was awarded 'Best Restaurant in the World' in 2018, is the legendary gem of Italian gastronomy in the hands of talented chef Massimo Bottura. Behind the pink façade in a peaceful Modena street, the dining space is made up of three elegant rooms adorned with contemporary artworks selected by Bottura and his wife, Lara. Throughout the colourful and sensational menu, the exuberant and charismatic chef weaves narratives and plays with traditions, experimenting with ingredients from the Emilia-Romagna region. Bottura's most famous courses include the 'Five Ages of Parmigiano Reggiano', which takes the diner through the region's esteemed cheeses (different temperatures, textures and tastes), and 'The Crunchy Part of the Lasagna', the chef's reinvention of a corner of the classic Italian dish. 'Caesar salad in Emilia' may look like naked lettuce, but hides 15 ingredients inside, such as cheese in the form of crispy wafers, eggs cured in salt and sugar and air-dried until they are hard enough to grate, and tomatoes strained through cheesecloth for 12 hours. Massimo and Lara Bottura just opened a country inn named Casa Maria Luigia, right outside the village. They have also built up Food For Soul, a not-for-profit project to fight hunger and food waste.

www.osteriafrancescana.it

— 89 —
LE LOUIS XV-ALAIN DUCASSE

MONACO

Monaco
Hôtel de Paris, Place du Casino, 98000 Monaco

TRADITIONAL
FRENCH

◆ TO VISIT BEFORE YOU DIE BECAUSE

Enjoy a royalty dinner, next to Prince Albert and Princess Charlene, in a setting reminiscent of Versailles.

Chef Alain Ducasse is at the helm of an international French cooking empire from the traditional French bistro to the ultimate fine-dining venue. One of the haute couture restaurants, rewarded with three Michelin stars, is Le Louis XV-Alain Ducasse in Monaco. Located on the ground floor of the Hotel de Paris, with an extraordinary Murano glass chandelier composed of 700 handmade pieces, the interior of the restaurant set in light and gold gives way to a gorgeously landscaped terrace overlooking the yacht harbour and the royal palace. Since its opening, Le Louis XV-Alain Ducasse has been dedicated to the very best in terms of Mediterranean produce, which Ducasse describes as 'essential cuisine', including giant sea bass cooked flat and studded with marjoram, and Pyrenean lamb seasoned with Espelette peppers, roasted in a fireplace.

RUSSIA	**Moscow** Smolenskaya Square 3, Moscow	MODERN RUSSIAN

◆ TO VISIT BEFORE YOU DIE BECAUSE

Here you can enjoy a unique gastronomical performance by chef Vladimir Mukhin, alongside stunning views of Moscow.

Located on the sixteenth floor of Smolenskava Square, White Rabbit embraces a whimsical Alice in Wonderland theme and a glass dome provides diners with a spectacular 360-degree view of the beautiful city. Hailing from five generations of cooks, chef Vladimir Mukhin is on a mission to export haute Russian food, founded on traditional recipes and ingredients, to the world, and to be in the vanguard of a new wave of young Russian culinary talents. He selects seasonal local products, original recipes and finely designed combinations, such as Black Sea oysters, rapa whelk from Yalta, Crimean truffle and other delicacies of contemporary Russian cuisine. His menu standouts include his 'orange dish' made of sea Buckthorn, sea urchin, and sea water, and a baked cabbage served with three different kinds of caviars.

whiterabbitmoscow.ru

— 91 —
TWINS GARDEN

RUSSIA

Moscow
Strastnoy Blvd, 8, Moscow, 125009

FARM-TO-TABLE

◆ TO VISIT BEFORE YOU DIE BECAUSE

You just have to try the twins' dry, aged cabbage with pork fat made in their hidden vegetable lab.

Ivan and Sergey Berezutskiy are identical Russian twins, and chefs who are challenging the Traditional Russian cuisine. They have worked in some of the world's finest kitchens: Ivan at El Bulli and El Celler de Can Roca in Spain, and Sergey at Alinea in Chicago and Varvary in Moscow. Since they weren't 100% satisfied with the produce they were getting in the country, they created their own organic farm in Kaluga Region, producing

80% of the ingredients of their menu; the idea is for Twins Garden to ultimately become completely self-sufficient. In their restaurant in central Moscow, they playfully reinterpret Russian cuisine with modern techniques and are doing amazing work on vegetables and in the wines they are making in-house. Diners will enjoy honey infused with sea urchin and a burrata made of vegetable.

FRANCE

Noirmoutier-en-l'Île
5 Rue Marie Lemonnier, 85330 Noirmoutier-en-l'Île

MODERN
FRENCH

◆ TO VISIT BEFORE YOU DIE BECAUSE

You will taste exceptional seafood products in a remote paradise in the French department of Vendée.

Chef Alexandre Couillon, student of chefs Michel Guérard and Thierry Marx, was 22 years old when he and his wife, Céline, opened La Marine on the island of Noirmoutier. Today, with unobstructed views of the harbour and the sea and a contemporary black-and-white decor, La Marine is among the best restaurants in France, where the chef takes diners into a straightforward modern approach to French cuisine based on the products from the island and the natural surroundings. The menu, which is predominantly fish and seafood, includes scrambled eggs topped with sea urchin, and monkfish served with a spear of white asparagus, rounded off with a sauce made from smoked eel and pear.

alexandrecouillon.com

NORWAY	Oslo	MODERN
	Schweigaardsgt. 15b, 0191 Oslo	SCANDINAVIAN

◆ TO VISIT BEFORE YOU DIE BECAUSE

It is a privilege to have dinner at the chef's table next to the kitchen, which has a direct view of the chefs at work and the modern skyline of the Bjørvika neighbourhood of Oslo.

Maaemo, from the old Norse meaning 'Mother Earth', is Oslo's three-Michelin-starred restaurant run by head chef Esben Holmboe Bang. Born and raised in Copenhagen, he has spent most of his culinary career in Oslo, where he builds around its local produce a cuisine reflecting the changing seasons and raw nature of Norway. Growing up in a family that had a strong focus on agriculture and sustainability, he uses only organic, biodynamic or wild produce to create his progressive brand of Norwegian cuisine. A meal at Maaemo takes guests on a breathtaking culinary tour of Norway, from the temperate climes of the southerly Hvaler islands to the cold, pristine waters of the west coast and on to the expansive inland wilderness of Røros. In the eight-table restaurant, the menu is a pageant of dishes such as Norwegian langoustines with pine, traditional sour-cream porridge served with shavings of reindeer heart, and Røros butter ice cream with brown butter caramel.

FRANCE

Ouches
728 Route de Villerest, 42155 Ouches

TRADITIONAL
FRENCH

◆ TO VISIT BEFORE YOU DIE BECAUSE
The legendary cellar has one of the finest burgundy collections in France.

Following on from the restaurateur Jean-Baptiste Troisgros' work, his three sons became famous for being leading members of the Nouvelle Cuisine movement in France in the late 1960s and '70s that pushed for a lighter and more elegant haute cuisine. Together, they invented the legendary 'Saumon à l'oseille' dish and were awarded three Michelin stars in 1968, which the restaurant has held ever since. Solely in charge of Maison Troisgros since 1996, Michel Troisgros and his wife Marie-Pierre have been running the hotel and restaurant, which is now located in Ouches in the Loire countryside, on a 17-hectare estate, with dedication and passion. Expect traditional and technical French cuisine combined with inventiveness, such as 'mussels in drunkenness': a mixture of cockles, mussels and oysters hidden underneath deep-fried spiralis and crushed pepper berries, cooked by his eldest son César Troisgros who is now in charge of the kitchen.

troisgros.fr

— 95 —
L'ARPÈGE

Paris
84 Rue de Varenne, 75007 Paris

◆ TO VISIT BEFORE YOU DIE BECAUSE
Here you can meet the legendary French alchemist of vegetables.

Being a legend of French cooking, chef Alain Passard is above all amongst the top chefs who have remained at the pinnacle of global fine dining for decades. The unique chef, who worked with chef Alain Senderens, founded his own restaurant L'Arpège in 1986, naming it as a tribute to music, one of his other passions. The chef decorated this Parisian gem in an Art Deco style, with smooth leather armchairs, wooden wall panels and details in Lalique crystal. In 2001, he announced his restaurant would become primarily vegetarian, featuring the produce from his three organic gardens around France. Diners can expect in Passard's poetic plates only the very best of more than 500 varieties of vegetables grown by his team and delivered each morning, along with the finest selection of fish and meat: a carpaccio of thinly sliced radish with touches of parmesan, or a *mesclun* salad with crunchy pistachio *pralin*. On his ever-changing menu, the most famous dishes include his *chaud-froid d'oeuf*, showcasing a contrast between the warm, runny egg yolk from a farm in the Loire Valley of France, the sherry vinegar-infused whipped cream that he adds to the top, and colourful dumplings made of seasonal vegetables. For the most fortunate guests, private lunches can also be organised in his gardens.

www.alain-passard.com

FRANCE	**Paris** Carré des Champs-Elysées, 8 Avenue Dutuit, 75008 Paris	MODERN FRENCH

◆ TO VISIT BEFORE YOU DIE BECAUSE

Tasting the fabulous golden-brown crust brioche, made from pike, served with a sublime extraction sauce made of celeriac, is a must.

Housed in an eighteenth-century Napoléon III mansion built on the Champs Elysées, Pavillon Ledoyen boasts a history few French restaurants can rival. Accessible via majestic stairs with butterflies painted on the ceiling, the dining room on the first floor is infused by the sunlight from the surrounding windows. Yannick Alléno, the famous three-Michelin-star chef, has always believed that French cuisine draws its strength from its strong heritage. Conscious that the first chapter of *Le Guide Culinaire d'Escoffier* (1903) and French cooking is all about sauce, he pursued a new way of creating coherence and harmony on the plate, exploring reduction sauces, which he calls 'extractions'. He has developed a unique and revolutionary process of cryo-concentration to perfect flavours and textures, and his visionary approach combines technique, tradition and excellence with audacity. Expect a fabulous golden-brown crust brioche, made from pike, where the perfectly executed fish is almost like a mousse in texture, served with a sublime sauce made of celeriac, or sea urchin soup in a burnt grapefruit shell, paired with foie gras and an iodised granita. The omakase Japanese restaurant Abysse is downstairs, with its stunning, arty, contemporary decor.

— 97 —
SEPTIME

FRANCE

Paris
80 Rue de Charonne, 75011 Paris

MODERN FRENCH

◆ TO VISIT BEFORE YOU DIE BECAUSE

It is a wonderful experience to visit the team's other extensions in the area before dinner, and to enjoy the seafood-focused Clamato and the tiny natural wine bar Septime Cave.

Chef Bertrand Grebaut worked in the kitchens of chef Alain Passard's landmark restaurant Arpège before opening Septime, his contemporary restaurant in the 11th arrondissement in Paris, in partnership with his friend Théo Pourriat. Introducing a reflection of a farm-to-table table where the two friends would themselves like to eat, Septime is at the forefront of Parisian cooking modernity with a unique and affordable menu based upon seasonal and carefully selected terroir produce. In this simple rustic place, the young chef pairs turbot with Brussels sprouts, bacon and a sauce of mushrooms from Paris, and white asparagus with oysters, hazelnuts and clotted cream.

— 98 —
ALAIN DUCASSE
AT PLAZA ATHÉNÉE

Paris

FRANCE

Hôtel Plaza Athénée, 25 Avenue Montaigne, 75008 Paris

MODERN FRENCH

◆ TO VISIT BEFORE YOU DIE BECAUSE

It is an experience to taste the langoustine and caviar dish in an extraordinary futurist design with polished stainless-steel shells and a stunning Swarovski chandelier.

In 2014, the renowned chef Alain Ducasse decided to completely challenge the traditional definition of fine dining with a new approach focusing on healthy, environmentally friendly food inspired by his 'Naturalité' philosophy. In the restaurant and dining rooms stunningly decorated in a soft white, cream and beige palette, Ducasse, with chef Romain Meder, decided to celebrate vegetables, fish and shellfish, and grains, and to rewrite the menu based on sustainable, wild and mostly organic ingredients. All through the meal, cream, butter and sugar are used as sparingly as possible. Diners experience extraordinary new tastes, such as sliced bread with wax, the genius green puy lentils and Kristal caviar in smoked eel jelly, served with buckwheat blinis and raw cream, and Tarbouriech oysters heated with honey and pollen. Also not to be missed are pastry chef Jessica Préalpato's fruit desserts, in which each bite highlights different textures and flavours, revealing acidity, bitterness and sweetness.

— 99 —
LA TOUR D'ARGENT

FRANCE

Paris
15 Quai de la Tournelle, Paris

TRADITIONAL
FRENCH

◆ TO VISIT BEFORE YOU DIE BECAUSE

The dining setting is magical with wonderful views of Paris' vistas, the grey zinc rooftops, terracotta chimneys and the majestic Notre-Dame Cathedral on the River Seine.

Eating at La Tour d'Argent, with one of the most exclusive restaurant views in the world, is like dining on a flying carpet above the city. With its 400-year-old decor, this restaurant is a delightful time warp that has hosted the world's rich and famous for centuries. It is where chef Philippe Labbé interprets the legendary canard à la presse, the 'Caneton Tour d'Argent', a duck-based recipe from Normandy.

tourdargent.com

— 100 —
CLOWN BAR

FRANCE

Paris
114 Rue Amelot, 75011 Paris

MODERN
FRENCH

◆ TO VISIT BEFORE YOU DIE BECAUSE

Sharing classic dishes with a modern twist, in a beautiful, old circus decor is a unique experience.

Established more than 100 years ago, Clown Bar is the place where chefs Sven Chartier and Ewen Lemoigne have created a bistro in an iconic location, serving upscale, bistro cuisine through inventive, sharing plates and a natural-wine list. Surrounded by colourful, hand-painted clowns on ceramic tiles and an art-nouveau, floral ceiling, the panoramic sensory experience begins with the eyes. Chef Atsumi Sota recently turned the kitchen over to chef Axel Ayza Gallart from Saturne restaurant. The new head chef brilliantly creates a duck foie gras pithiviers, poached veal brains in a ponzu sauce, beef tartare, and smoked Burrata with pine nuts.

ITALY	**Rubano** Via Liguria 1, 35030 Rubano (PD)	MODERN ITALIAN

◆ TO VISIT BEFORE YOU DIE BECAUSE

Here you can experience the creations of the youngest chef in history to have been awarded three Michelin stars, while admiring his artworks on the walls of the dining room.

Le Calandre is situated on a busy road in the nondescript Italian town of Sarmeola di Rubano, outside Padua. The Alajmo brothers inherited the restaurant from their parents and turned it into a three-Michelin-star establishment. Massimiliano works in the kitchen, while his older brother, Raffaele, oversees the dining room and is in charge of the wines. Chef Massimiliano is the youngest chef in history to have been awarded three stars by the Michelin Guide after being trained in France to work with two of the country's most prominent chefs,

Marc Veyrat and Michel Guérard. Three tasting menus are available: one features the chef's classics, while the other two – 'Max' and 'Raf' – offer a window onto the brothers' own tastes. Combining an artist's eye with a chef's deft technique and extremely sensitive palate, Massimiliano Alajmo has definitely elevated Le Calandre's cuisine to the highest level, with the right balance of tradition and modernity. Must-try dishes include saffron, juniper and liquorice powder risotto, and crispy buffalo ricotta and mozzarella cannelloni with tomato sauce.

— 102 —
ARZAK

SPAIN

San Sebastián
Avenida Alcalde Elósegui 273,
20015 Donostia, San Sebastián

MODERN BASQUE

◆ TO VISIT BEFORE YOU DIE BECAUSE

It is beautiful and quite unique to watch a father and daughter combination in a kitchen.

Situated at the top of a hill in San Sebastián, this restaurant has been in the Arzak family for generations. It was charismatic chef Juan Mari, now 76 years old, who revived the menu to make it what it is today after stints working with chefs Paul Bocuse and Pierre Troisgros. As the creator of the New Basque Cuisine, the culinary concept born in the 1970s, he was the second chef in Spain to receive three Michelin stars. In the main dining room, which has impressions of forks and spoons on the walls and tables dressed in white linen, diners receive the warmest welcome from the venerable chef while his talented daughter, Elena Mari, runs daily operations. Father and daughter create stunning dishes, which are avant-garde yet rooted in Basque traditions, such as sardines paired with strawberries, lobster with citrus and hemp mustard, and sea bass served on top of a tablet computer with moving images of the sea. A special feature of many of the dishes is the crunchy element: for example, Big Chocolate Truffle with candyfloss, cacao and chocolate. Upstairs, those with curious minds will discover a tiny second kitchen, which is the restaurant's research lab, and a room containing a library of 1,400 spices and other ingredients, such as Vietnamese green rice, dry seaweeds and vanilla-scented tonka beans.

— 103 —
EKSTEDT

SWEDEN

Stockholm
Humlegårdsgatan 17, 11446 Stockholm

**OPEN
FIRE**

◆ TO VISIT BEFORE YOU DIE BECAUSE

Here you can experience a primal and radical return to ancient cooking with no electricity.

After growing up in a small village in northern Sweden where life revolved around the great outdoors, chef Niklas Ekstedt's early training at El Bulli in Spain and Charlie Trotter's in the USA has helped ensure his culinary creativity burns bright. Moving back to Stockholm, he created an open kitchen featuring a wood and metallic decor with industrial lamps, where the ambience is warm and the chefs clad in blacksmith-style leather aprons toil away at the flames. This is the place where Ekstedt chose to revitalise traditional Scandinavian cooking techniques, ditching electricity and gas in favour of burning wood, and working with local and seasonal ingredients to produce dishes such as a diced reindeer heart with mushrooms, lingonberry, butter and fresh herbs served in a freshly made tortilla, and sweetbreads cooked in hay and juniper.

— 104 —
FRANTZÉN

SWEDEN

Stockholm
Klara Norra kyrkogata 26,
11122 Stockholm

**CHEF'S
COUNTER**

◆ TO VISIT BEFORE YOU DIE BECAUSE
Here you can have one of the best Swedish dining experiences,
in a more than intimate place.

Frantzén is one of Sweden's most celebrated restaurants and is located in a three-storey space in a nineteenth-century building. Chef Björn Frantzén was a professional football player before starting his career as an award-winning chef. Beginning his journey as a chef in the Swedish army, he has worked at other Michelin-starred restaurants specialising in classic French cuisine, such as Alain Passard's three-Michelin-starred L'Arpège in Paris. The discreet entrance leads visitors into a waiting room, where ageing cabinets contain hanging hunks of meat, they enter the lift and hear David Bowie soundtracks. Downstairs, in the dining room, the chefs cook on an open fire in the kitchen, carefully assembling several hundred Nordic ingredients for 23 covers a night. The chef's technique is classically French, but the ingredients and cooking are unmistakably Swedish: buttery sauce of fermented white asparagus and beurre noisette is spooned over turbot with Frantzén 'reserve caviar' placed on top, and the expertly cooked liquorice-glazed veal sweetbreads are served with anise herbs, lemon peel, caramelised onion, roasted onion velouté and toasted almond milk. Some Japanese influences can be detected in the fermented garlic and lemon peel, and konbu and liquorice.

— 105 —
OAXEN KROG

SWEDEN

Stockholm
Beckholmsvägen 26, SE-11521 Stockholm

**MODERN
SCANDINAVIAN**

◆ TO VISIT BEFORE YOU DIE BECAUSE

Here you can enjoy the amazing beer and syrup bread, and then fall asleep on the restaurant owners' hotel ship called the Prince van Orangiën, built in 1935 in the Netherlands.

Seventeen years ago, the couple Magnus Ek and Agneta Green founded a small restaurant on the island of Oaxen in Stockholm's archipelago, where they served inventive dishes using island produce and herbs. Because of the island's harsh weather, Oaxen Krog was closed for much of the year. Therefore, they decided to relocate their restaurant to the island of Djurgården in central Stockholm, where they entirely rebuilt the shipyard so that the nautical spirit of their place could remain intact. The walls and ceiling of the dining room are covered in slatted oak panels, and the tables have been custom-made by shipyard carpenters, paired with a 1950s chair design. All ingredients are sourced in Scandinavia and during the summer season the kitchen staff picks wild herbs and plants on Djurgården island to create the beautiful dishes of this internationally acclaimed gourmet restaurant.

oaxen.com

— 106 —
MAISON PIC

FRANCE

Valence
285 Avenue Victor-Hugo, 26000 Valence

MODERN
FRENCH

◆ TO VISIT BEFORE YOU DIE BECAUSE

You would meet the only female chef in France in the last 50 years to hold three Michelin stars.

Anne-Sophie Pic is the only female chef in France in the last 50 years to hold three Michelin stars and is part of French culinary history. She grew up in Valence with an intuitive love of gastronomy, surrounded by the notion of good food thanks to her father, Jacques Pic, and grandfather, André Pic, both of whom were chefs. After beginning her career in management, Anne-Sophie Pic realised her dream and followed in the footsteps of the men in her family to assume leadership of her family's restaurant, Maison Pic. Once she had succeeded in regaining the third Michelin star, which was lost a few years after her father passed away, she worked for ten years to develop her own style of cooking, with light, intensely flavoured sauces that combine unexpected flavours. In the modern minimalist decor of her white kitchen overlooking a Japanese garden, Pic prepares soft-boiled eggs with wild mushrooms and discusses the complexity of flavours with expert 'noses' from the world of scent. Whereas her father served his sea bass in a rich cream sauce and coated with caviar, hers comes with a light mushroom, ginger and rose-geranium sauce, with its scents and flavours revealing themselves one at a time.

www.anne-sophie-pic.com

— 107 —
AMAN

ITALY

Venice
Palazzo Papadopoli, Calle Tiepolo 1364,
Sestiere San Polo, Venice 30125

**TRADITIONAL
ITALIAN**

◆ TO VISIT BEFORE YOU DIE BECAUSE

It is romantic to start the evening with a Bellini at the rooftop bar of the hotel, with views of the sunset over the lagoon.

The Aman Hotel is housed in the unique setting of Palazzo Papadopoli, which features Murano glass chandeliers and ceilings painted by the eighteenth-century master Giovanni Battista Tiepolo. The hotel boasts 24 lavishly appointed suites and a restaurant. In an incredibly refined and romantic interior, diners look out directly over the Grand Canal with a menu including fish caught in the nearby lagoon and vegetables from the local market, in classical and elegant Italian dishes such as a wonderfully crunchy artichoke salad with pecorino cheese, tagliolini with white truffles and zabaione flavoured with passito wine.

— 108 —
QUADRI

ITALY

Venice
Piazza San Marco 121, 30124 Venice

MODERN ITALIAN

◆ TO VISIT BEFORE YOU DIE BECAUSE

This would be the ideal place to make a marriage proposal,
while sipping a glass of Italian sparkling wine,
and overlooking the legendary St Mark's Square.

The Alajmo family, fifth-generation chefs and restaurateurs, runs this eighteenth-century restaurant situated behind the arches of the arcade in St Mark's Square. Located on the first floor of the building, Quadri has a unique setting and was restored in early 2018 by Philippe Starck and a team of Venetian artisans, which brought back the original splendour and poetry of the space but in a modern context. With a stunning view of the Duomo, Quadri has a cuisine that represents a contemporary expression of traditional Italian and Venetian cuisine, with fish, fruit and vegetables that arrive fresh every day from the Rialto market. Tiny raw shrimps are served with fried artichokes and an emulsion made with just pistachios, tarragon and water, and the roasted suckling pig is plated with perfect mashed potatoes and a generous grating of white truffle.

www.alajmo.it/en/sezione/ristorante-quadri/ristorante-quadri

— 109 —
HARRY'S BAR

ITALY

Venice
San Marco, 1322, 30124 Venice VE

TRADITIONAL ITALIAN

◆ TO VISIT BEFORE YOU DIE BECAUSE

Here you can drink a Bellini, the bar's famous creation of white peach juice and sparkling wine, while eating great Italian classics in a 30s untouched atmosphere.

The most renowned bar and restaurant in Venice, Harry's Bar, was founded in 1930 by the Cipriani family. Both regulars and tourists are meeting all year long at this legendary place where Ernest Hemingway used to sip coffee on Sunday afternoons. In the intimate atmosphere with old-style wooden trim and comfy seats, elegant waiters serve what can be called 'legendary', as there are few restaurants on the planet that have invented both a famous cocktail and a dish. The Bellini, of course, which is a mixture of fresh white peaches crushed with sparkling Prosecco, and the Carpaccio, the thinly sliced beef served with a fine line of mayonnaise mixed with lemon juice on the top, invented for Contessa Amalia Nani Mocenigo, whom the doctor had put on a strictly raw meat diet. The waiters seem to have been there forever, dressed in white tuxedos and serving elegant Italian classics, precisely executed, such as squid dishes, pasta and veal Milanese. For a timeless atmosphere, Harry's Bar is not to be missed.

cipriani.com/restaurant/?loc=venice-harrys-bar

THE NETHERLANDS	Zwolle	MODERN DUTCH
	Spinhuisplein 1, 8011 Zwolle	

◆ TO VISIT BEFORE YOU DIE BECAUSE

You may be lucky enough to have dinner at the exclusive table in the kitchen itself, where you will experience at close quarters the extreme creativity and imagination of the chef, Jonnie Boer.

Located 75 miles (120 kilometres) north-east of Amsterdam in Zwolle village, set in the depths of a fifteenth-century Dominican monastery boasting magnificent gothic leaded windows, De Libije offers an extraordinary gastronomic experience. Chef Jonnie Boer is praised worldwide for his creativity and terroir-based kitchen, mixing local food and cutting-edge techniques. The menu is tailored to suit individual diners' specific tastes, where they select four dishes from different colour-coded sections before further plates are added to create the whole menu. The beef tartare and oyster canapés are assembled directly onto the back of your hand, the dry-aged dairy beef is then seared on hot rocks at the table and served with smoked eel and braised lemon, and the langoustines are marinated for three hours in a kombucha, slightly charred at the table, and finished with a salad of bamboo, Japanese pear, galangal, turmeric and a jus of French beans.

— 111 —
THE TEST KITCHEN

Cape Town
375 Albert Road, Woodstock, Cape Town, 7915

◆ TO VISIT BEFORE YOU DIE BECAUSE

You can start your meal with a rhubarb-and-custard negroni or a smoky Old Fashioned cocktail made with lapsang souchong.

Chef Luke Dale-Roberts was born in rural England and had an active youth, fishing and spending hours outdoor in the countryside. Working in the UK, Bali, South Korea and Japan opened his eyes to a world of techniques and ingredients, which he now adopts at his restaurant through food based on popular global dishes with a South African twist. The Test Kitchen, located in The Old Biscuit Mill, is known for its cuisine and its two intimate dining areas: one 'dark', where diners receive their first seven courses, and one 'light', where the rest of the fine-dining menu is served in an industrial setting. The menu is a map presented as a scroll, showing the culinary journey diners will make, from Peru to Japan and back down to South Africa, with a ceviche with the chef's trademark stamp and a herbaceous stinging-nettle granita, savoury billionaire's shortbread made with chilli, dark chocolate and duck, and baby garden vegetables to be grasped by their green tails and dipped into a creamy ssamjang paste sprinkled with crispy onion dust.

www.thetestkitchen.co.za

— 112 —
GAGGAN

THAILAND

Bangkok
68/1 Soi Langsuan, Ploenchit Road,
Lumpini, Bangkok 10330

MODERN ASIAN

◆ TO VISIT BEFORE YOU DIE BECAUSE

Here you can taste chef Gaggan Anand's curry dish 'Lick It Up', named after a song by the American rock band Kiss, which you lick directly from the plate.

Gaggan Anand is one of a kind. In his lab upstairs in his colonial house in Bangkok, this rebel chef born in India, who likes loud music, redefines his native food through what he calls 'progressive Indian cuisine'. Taking influences from all over the world, the menu of 25 bites inspired by the emoticons on smartphones includes Mexican-inspired taco bites, Japanese-Indian nigiri sushi and aubergine Oreo biscuits. The classic 'Yoghurt Explosion', inspired by chef Ferran Adrià's spherical olives, but with an Indian spice twist, remains on the menu alongside newer signatures such as 'Lick It Up', where diners are encouraged to lick a flavoursome curry straight from the plate. The chef has pledged to close his flagship restaurant in 2020 to open a small place in Fukuoka, Japan, with fellow chef Takeshi 'Goh' Fukuyama of La Maison de la Nature Goh.

eatatgaggan.com

THAILAND	**Bangkok** 27 South Sathorn Road, Tungmahamek, Sathorn, Bangkok 10120	MODERN THAI

◆ TO VISIT BEFORE YOU DIE BECAUSE

The wonderful crab curry is the best in town.

Located on the ground floor of the Metropolitan Hotel on Sathorn Road in Bangkok, Nahm has a decor that combines a tasteful mix of Thai-styled brick columns and latticed wooden screens in a soothing modern atmosphere. Nahm's cuisine, formerly executed by famous chef David Thompson, has been under the guidance of chef Pim Techamuanvivit since May 2018, and her new dishes have stayed true to Nahm's original vision of authentic Thai cuisine, while also bringing a renewed focus on closer relationships with farmers and artisian food producers across Thailand to ensure only the most exceptional produce makes it onto the menu. To reflect nineteenth-century Thai royal gastronomy, the pinnacle of Thai cooking, chef Pim Techamuanvivit elegantly combines the freshness of products grown by local farmers and the power of carefully chosen spices. Try the blue swimmer crab, coriander and pickled garlic on rice crackers with peanuts, or the miang of lobster.

THAILAND	**Bangkok** 3rd Floor, Gaysorn, 999 Ploenchit Road, Lumpini, Bangkok	MODERN THAI

◆ TO VISIT BEFORE YOU DIE BECAUSE

The roasted duck with a myriad of Thai herbs and spices coupled with the crunch of the rice crackers is a must-try.

In order to bring new attention to forgotten Thai recipes, chefs Jason Bailey and Bee Satongun have combed through old cookery books from the period of King Rama V to King Rama VII (roughly 1870–1930) and have scoured the countryside for the right ingredients. They follow the authentic textures and flavours of Thai cuisine and presents them in sophisticated tasting menus, which introduce rare herbs and ingredients, from edible hummingbird flowers in the smoky southern yellow curry with red spanner crab, to salt from Nan province. The ancient Thai recipes, and the unique and organic ingredients, are combined with modern presentation, as exemplified by signature dishes such as stock-poached organic pork served with basil, coriander, red grapefruit, avocado, toasted rice and local flowers.

www.pastebangkok.com

— 115 —
SRA BUA BY KIIN KIIN

THAILAND

Bangkok
Siam Kempinski Hotel Bangkok,
Rama 1 Road 991/9, 10330 Bangkok

MODERN THAI

◆ TO VISIT BEFORE YOU DIE BECAUSE

This is the place to try the lobster locked inside gelatinous pearls that melt in the mouth with a sip of Tom Yam broth.

Located in the luxurious Siam Kempinski Hotel Bangkok, Sra Bua by Kiin Kiin is the concept of renowned chef Henrik Yde-Andersen, whose Kiin Kiin restaurant in Copenhagen is one of the world's very few Thai restaurants with a Michelin star rating. Behind Sra Bua by Kiin Kiin's exquisitely composed food presentation and global cooking techniques, the familiar flavours of traditional Thai dishes are well maintained. Within the attractive main dining room made from traditional teak wood, Sra Bua offers molecular gastronomy with progressive interpretations of long-established Thai dishes, such as frozen red curry with lobster salad or curry soup served in ice cream cones, plump Hokkaido scallops with zesty tamarind and lemongrass sauce, and cod in green curry. The luxurious signature banana cake with salted ice cream and caramelised milk should not be missed.

srabuabykiinkiin.com

— 116 —
SÜHRING

THAILAND

Bangkok
10, Yen Akat Soi 3, Chongnonsi,
Yannawa, Bangkok 10120

MODERN GERMAN

◆ TO VISIT BEFORE YOU DIE BECAUSE

Here you can escape from Bangkok chaos to experience refined German food in a peaceful villa.

The German twin chefs Thomas and Mathias Sühring opened their restaurant in Bangkok after years of working in their native Germany, the Netherlands and Italy. Located in a 1970s villa in the heart of the Sathorn neighbourhood in Bangkok, the restaurant has German tasting menus and seasonal dishes that are primarily inspired by their home country, their childhood memories and family recipes. Having received two Michelin stars, Sühring is worth the excursion, and it is one of the most delightful places in the city.

— 117 —
TAWLET

Beirut
Beirut, Sector 79 – Naher Street 12
(Jisr el-Hadeed), Chalhoub Building 22

**TRADITIONAL
LEBANESE**

◆ TO VISIT BEFORE YOU DIE BECAUSE

Here you can try real Lebanese soul food, made from real local people, thanks to Kamal Mouzawak's wonderful social project.

In Beirut, a city in which food is a focal point of society, founder and owner Kamal Mouzawak has been using food to bring people together for years, in a wider human development project. He organised the city's first farmers' market, called Souk el Tayeb, and later he opened a collective cultural restaurant: Tawlet. Open only at lunch time, Tawlet, which means 'table' in Arabic, is a beautiful modern restaurant located in the heart of Beirut's trendy Mar Mikhael district. Each week, women from different areas of Lebanon cook together in the open kitchen and share the history and traditions of their own region through food. The project has a single human purpose: to create social and culinary bonds through the sharing of food.

— 118 —
AMBER

CHINA

Hong Kong

7/F, The Landmark Mandarin Oriental, The Landmark,
15 Queen's Road Central, Hong Kong

MODERN
EUROPEAN

◆ TO VISIT BEFORE YOU DIE BECAUSE

At Amber you can experience elegant European cooking in one of Hong Kong's most refined hotels.

Located in one of Hong Kong's most luxurious and distinctive five-star hotels, the Landmark Mandarin Oriental, Amber stands out for its floor-to-ceiling glass window offering a beautiful panorama of the city. Dutch chef Richard Ekkebus, the executive chef and culinary director of the place, honed his craft with French culinary legends including Alain Passard and Pierre Gagnaire. Throughout his cuisine, his main focus is on superior produce and ingredients sourced from all parts of the world, with modern twists, textures and colours, such as the duck foie gras poached in mushroom tea or ebisu oysters coagulated at 70°C. Ekkebus is currently working to create a movement in Hong Kong to reduce the use of plastic in restaurants, and to recycle oils into biofuels. His intention is to grow a roof garden on top of the building, with herbs and flowers to initiate the first footsteps of sustainability in Hong Kong.

www.amberhongkong.com

LUNG KING HEEN

CHINA

Hong Kong

8 Finance Street, Central, Hong Kong

CLASSICAL
CANTONESE

◆ TO VISIT BEFORE YOU DIE BECAUSE

The three-star Cantonese food of chef Chan Yan Tak is served in front of the stunning views of Victoria Harbour and Hong Kong's skyscrapers.

The restaurant Lung King Heen, which translates as 'view of the dragon', is located in the Four Seasons Hotel and was the first Chinese restaurant to be awarded three Michelin stars: the result of its combination of ground-breakingly good food and spectacular views of Victoria Harbour. Born in Kowloon, chef Chan Yan Tak is a world-renowned master of Cantonese cuisine. His brainchilds are the baked whole abalone puffs with diced chicken, a popular dim sum dish that has inspired other restaurants to create their own versions, barbecued suckling pig, braised goose webs with Chinese mushrooms in a casserole, and crispy pork ribs with osmanthus and pear. Diners should book well in advance for the popular dim sum, which is available only at lunchtime.

— 120 —
MOTT 32

Hong Kong

Standard Chartered Bank Building,
4–4a Des Voeux Road, Central, Hong Kong

MODERN
CHINESE

◆ TO VISIT BEFORE YOU DIE BECAUSE

The tender apple wood-roasted 42-day Peking duck, served with thin pancakes, is a must-eat that has to be pre-ordered 48 hours in advance.

People enter another world when they descend Mott 32's spiral staircase into a stylish industrial dining room, in the basement of the Standard Chartered Bank building in central Hong Kong. The food is a modern take on mainly Cantonese specialties, along with a few Sichuan and Beijing dishes, all using first-rate ingredients. In one of the glamorous dark rooms, with mirrors and oriental papers on the walls, diners will settle in leather and velvet banquettes to enjoy sweet crusted pork buns or the char siu pork that arrives crackling at the table with a light and crispy sugar-coated skin, giving way to an incredibly soft and fragrant Iberico meat.

www.mott32.com

— 121 —
NEIGHBORHOOD

Hong Kong
61-63 Hollywood Road, Hong Kong

MODERN
EUROPEAN

◆ TO VISIT BEFORE YOU DIE BECAUSE

Neighborhood promises a special night out with friends, eating magically tasty food in a casual setting.

At his cosy restaurant, Neighborhood, chef David Lai provides an escape from the chaos of the city in order to experience an unusual, exciting and spectacular culinary moment. Hong Kong-born chef David Lai's love for cooking began in San Francisco's Bay area while working in a restaurant to help support his art history and fine arts degree at The University of California in Berkeley, later to continue at Alain Ducasse's restaurants in Monaco and Hong Kong. His artistic skills made a natural transition into the culinary world, focusing on both seafood and local produce in a neighbourhood bistro format with a consistently changing daily menu. He uses the seasonality and freshness of the produce, mixing French and Italian influences with ingredients that are thoughtfully sourced, well-priced and providing small surprises here and there. Highlights include the 'bouillabaisse' with the fish of the day, bone marrow and kale risotto, and bouchot mussels in a green-curry broth.

www.facebook.com/neighborhoodhk/

— 122 —
BELON

CHINA

Hong Kong
41 Elgin Street, Soho, Hong Kong

TRADITIONAL FRENCH

◆ TO VISIT BEFORE YOU DIE BECAUSE

Here you can taste chef Daniel Calvert's exceptional pithiviers, a traditional pie from France, which he fills with pigeon, fig and Amaretto.

Named after the famous French oyster traditionally found in Brittany, Belon boldly mixes stylish Hong Kong strip with bustling Paris bistro in the Soho district. With large and comfortable banquettes, the atmosphere is elegant, yet relaxed. Chef Daniel Calvert has spent 10 years in Michelin-starred kitchens, such as Per Se in New York and Le Bristol's Epicure in Paris, before heading to Hong Kong to take part in the young, exciting scene of the city. In this place where simplicity and service are the keywords, Daniel Calvert delights in adding a contemporary touch to the classics of French cuisine, which he prepares with the most exceptional, quality products such as a home-made leavened bread with salted, Channel Island butter, a pork and pistachio terrine with Dijon mustard and celery roots with truffles.

— 123 —
SONEVA KIRI

**THAILAND
(KO KUT)**

Koh Kood
110 Moo 4, Koh Kood Sub-District,
Koh Kood District, Trat 23000

**TRADITIONAL
THAI**

◆ TO VISIT BEFORE YOU DIE BECAUSE

A candlelit dinner in a private bamboo pod hanging 16 feet
off the ground is an experience.

Situated on Koh Kood, the fourth largest island off the coast of Thailand, Soneva Kiri is a remote eco-resort with private luxury villas where guests come to snorkel on the reefs, explore the rainforest, or stargaze in the property's observatory. In this paradise setting, the tree house experience is taken to the next level: guests can dine in a eucalyptus tree 16 feet above the rainforest, sitting comfortably in a steel and rattan pod, overlooking the Gulf of Thailand, while a 'flying waiter' is attached to a zip wire to serve them. Chef Khun Benz prepares authentic Thai meals based on the freshest catch of the day and the products available in the local markets or the resort's organic garden. The menu includes the playfully named 'canapés in the canopy': crispy sweet potato, banana and taro chips, or galangal-baked white fish in banana leaves with lime and a fresh salsa verde.

www.soneva.com/soneva-kiri

— 124 —
MASQUE MUMBAI

Mumbai

INDIA

Unit G3, Laxmi Woollen Mills, Shakti Mills Lane,
off Dr E. Moses Road, Mahalaxmi, Mumbai 400011

MODERN
INDIAN

◆ TO VISIT BEFORE YOU DIE BECAUSE
This is the first farm-to-table dining experience in India.

Masque is an ingredient-driven restaurant set in Mumbai's former industrial mill area that offers a ten-course chef's tasting menu, the first of its kind in India. Inspired by the modernisation of Mumbai's mill lands, the space manages to consciously disregard its own grandeur, with mute colours and textures, lighting in the form of bulbs and marbles. The food is based on the farm-to-table concept, by which restaurants eliminate the middle vendors and purchase directly from farms, so focusing on locally produced and fresher ingredients. For 20 months, owner Aditi Dugar, and the Kashmir-born head chef Prateek Sadhu, whose previous work includes stints at Alinea, French Laundy, Le Bernadin and Noma, scoured the subcontinent to find reliable sources for every ingredient they wished to serve: cheese comes from a small town in Andhra Pradesh, olive oil from Rajasthan, goats' milk from Bangalore and fish from the Andaman Islands. Kashmir is an important influence on Prateek's cooking. Traditional foods are prepared in new ways, where the focus is on putting what is essential on the plate, and bringing out singular, but familiar, flavours.

150 RESTAURANTS YOU NEED TO VISIT BEFORE YOU DIE

NAMA AT AMANPULO

PHILIPPINES

Pamalican Island
Pamalican Island, Sulu Archipelago, Palawan

TRADITIONAL JAPANESE

◆ TO VISIT BEFORE YOU DIE BECAUSE

It is rare to be able to taste such exceptional sushi, with your feet in the sand.

On the remote reef-fringed Pamalican Island in the Philippines, Amanpulo offers a Crusoe luxury retreat with snow-white beaches and crystal-clear seas. A few steps from the beach, its restaurant Nama celebrates Japanese influences with authentic, uncomplicated and elegant dishes that champion locally sourced produce. Amanpulo has its own organic garden that supplies many of the restaurant's ingredients, while fresh seafood is provided by local fishermen, or sourced from Japan. On the menu, sushi, nigiri sushi and sashimi are available alongside signature dishes such as Kobe gyu, a Japanese Kobe Wagyu steak grilled at the table over charcoal and served with Moshio mineral salt, a seaweed infused salt produced by the ancient Japanese nearly 2,500 years ago.

SOUTH KOREA	Seoul 56, Ujeongguk-ro, Jongno-gu, Seoul	VEGETARIAN/ KOREAN

◆ TO VISIT BEFORE YOU DIE BECAUSE

Thanks to chef Jeong Kwan's philosophy, eating vegetables has never been as spiritual as in this Buddhist temple.

Although not a chef or restaurant in the traditional sense, Jeong Kwan and her cooking at Baekyangsa Temple in the Naejangsan National Park, about four hours south of Seoul, have inspired some of the world's most celebrated chefs. Building on Buddhist philosophy and drawing for inspiration on her own gardens, for her, food is meant to nourish your body and help your mind find enlightenment, and is a way of bringing humans back to nature and clearing their minds for meditation. On this precious little patch of land, Kwan quietly cultivates her plants and cooks for the monks based down the hill. She creates astonishing vegan dishes by cooking the vegetables in doenjang (fermented bean paste, called 'Korean Miso'), soy sauce and syrups (berries and plums fermented with sugar, for three to five years), and combining them with gochugaru and sesame and perilla seeds.

baekyangsa.kr

SOUTH KOREA

Seoul

Gangnam-gu, Nonhyun-dong 94-9, 1st floor, Seoul

MODERN KOREAN

◆ TO VISIT BEFORE YOU DIE BECAUSE

The crème brûlée trio made with traditional Korean sauces offers your palate flavours like no other.

Chef Mingoo Kang trained under Martin Berasategui in San Sebastián, and at Nobu in Miami and the Bahamas. From these culinary experiences Kang created Mingles, which is undoubtedly one of the most interesting modern Korean restaurants in the Gangnam area of Seoul, mixing Japanese, Spanish and French influences with Korean cuisine.

Choosing seasonal ingredients and recipes that have been passed down through palace kitchens over hundreds of years, the chef creates impressive combinations, such as egg custard with sansho pepper, with hints of chorizo and sansho pepper at the top, and a silky soft-boiled egg yolk surrounded by egg-white foam and cauliflower below.

— 128 —
ULTRAVIOLET BY PAUL PAIRET

Shanghai
Waitan, District de Huangpu, Shanghai

MODERN
INVENTIVE

◆ TO VISIT BEFORE YOU DIE BECAUSE

Here you can experience chef Paul Pairet's excellent menu with precisely choreographed audio, visual, scent and mood for every course. It ensures a sensational memory.

Set in an anonymous bunker on the outskirts of central Shanghai, Ultraviolet by Paul Pairet is considered by many to be the most avant-garde restaurant experience in the world. Diners are driven to the secret location, which is down a dark alleyway in an industrial warehouse space. The dimly lit dining room is furnished with five chairs set on either side of a communal dining table, with no window. Inside this futuristic set-up, only ten guests per night experience the ultimate 20-course menus

'UVA', 'UVB' and 'UVC', which combine technology such as video, audio, bespoke lighting and scents with the dishes and drinks to stimulate all the senses, challenge expectations and trick the eye. During the meal a 360-degree screen shows seashell images accompanied by dramatic music, while ten waiters dressed in grey uniforms and baseball caps serve exquisite wood-fired abalone on silver plates. Soon after, a picnic of fish, rice and fennel is served in metal containers on a grassy knoll, with birdsong and the scent of freshly cut grass.

uvbypp.cc

— 129 —
FU HE HUI

Shanghai

CHINA

1037 Yuyuan Road, Changing District,
Shanghai 200050

VEGETARIAN

TO VISIT BEFORE YOU DIE BECAUSE

Here you can experience an exquisitely refined vegetable experience, through the smooth, mashed-taro dumplings with a textured exterior that crackles delightfully in the mouth, as well as one of the most exceptional tea pairings with your meal.

Fortune, Harmony and Wisdom. These three words are the translations of the three characters adorning this Zen, colonial townhouse situated in the middle of Shanghai. Within a three-storey structure with furniture and art pieces from the Ming and Qing Dynasties, Fu He Hui in Shanghai is a temple of vegetarian Chinese cuisine that proves vegetables are more than a way of eating; they are a way of living. All through the fine-dining menu, Chef Tony Lu makes each dish of vegetables an experience in itself, where the identity and essence of each ingredient is put forward in a very creative way ranging from stir-fried lily bulb with asparagus and elm-ear mushrooms to seared king oyster mushrooms with tofu skin, served on a mandarin pancake.

BURNT ENDS

SINGAPORE

Singapore
20 Teck Lim Road, Singapore 088391

OPEN FIRE/
CHEF'S
COUNTER

◆ TO VISIT BEFORE YOU DIE BECAUSE

The Burnt Ends Sanger – two warm and fluffy brioche buns with a generous amount of cheese spread onto the top bun, and a smoky juicy ten-hour pulled pork shoulder – is not to be missed.

Located on Teck Lim Road near Chinatown, the restaurant's industrial-looking dining room is dominated by a four-ton, double-cavity wood-burning brick kiln. Chef David Pynt learnt the basics of his craft with legendary Spanish fire master Victor Arguinzoniz at Etxebarri in the Basque Country. At Burnt Ends, Pynt cooks at the counter some of the best Australian and Western cuisine in Singapore, serving a collection of dishes from fresh seafood to juicy roast meat touched by the kiln's heat and smoke, and by the custom grills, raising and lowering them to ensure the correct temperature levels. Diners can expect grilled Australian langoustines with tobiko and a kombu beurre blanc, charred fennel paired with fresh orange and burrata, or onglet steak with burnt onion and bone marrow.

SINGAPORE	Singapore	MODERN
	1 St Andrew's Road, 01-04 National Gallery, Singapore 178957	FRENCH

◆ TO VISIT BEFORE YOU DIE BECAUSE

Odette has the most exceptional dining room, and chef Julien Royer cooks one of the finest dining cuisines in Singapore.

With a feminine soft pink, grey and cream colour scheme and beautiful artworks, restaurant Odette is a modern French restaurant located at the National Art Gallery in Singapore. Chef Julien Royer worked for Michel Bras in France, Antonin Bonnet in London and at Jaan in Singapore before opening his own restaurant and earning two Michelin stars within a year. Named after his grandmother, Odette pays homage to her, celebrating the fond memories and nostalgia that have inspired his food. In his restaurant, Royer's aim is to offer the warm comforts of home and communal eating within a timeless setting through a cooking style he describes as 'essential cuisine': the very best seasonal ingredients and artisan produce from around the world are put centre stage in elegant and refined dishes. Diners can expect beautifully colourful dishes such as a French guinea fowl served with celeriac risotto and foie gras croquette, or trout with grilled octopus and romanesco broccoli, splashed with miso caramel.

www.odetterestaurant.com

— 132 —
MUME

TAIWAN

Taipei
28, Siwei Rd, Da'an District,
Taipei City

**MODERN
TAIWANESE**

◆ TO VISIT BEFORE YOU DIE BECAUSE

Here you can experience some Nordic influences combined with the beauty of Taiwanese ingredients.

Mume is the word for plum blossom, Taiwan's national flower. The restaurant offers a chic modern decor with an extensive cocktail bar at the front, and a dining area with an open kitchen at the back. Strongly influenced by Noma (Copenhagen), with herbs and flowers decorating the dishes, Hong Kong-born chef Richie Lin, Australian chef Kai Ward and American chef Long Xiong showcase the best ingredients the region has to offer to create their modern European casual fine-dining restaurant, with a Taiwanese terroir, constantly developing a deeper relationship with local producers. The results include burnt cabbage topped with smoked salmon roe and hazelnuts, ice-cold poached oysters served with a citrusy granita, pork ribs aged with miso and plum glaze, and a summer salad of nearly 30 different vegetables dressed with fermented black beans.

— 133 —
RAW

TAIWAN

Taipei
301, Le Qun 3rd Road, Taipei City

**MODERN
TAIWANESE**

◆ TO VISIT BEFORE YOU DIE BECAUSE

This is the hottest place on the island, opened by celebrity chef André Chiang who just moved back to the place of his childhood.

RAW is located in the Zhongshan District of Taipei, set into the curves of an innovative interior design made of Taiwanese pine. Opened by Taiwanese chef André Chiang, the restaurant goes back to his roots and has quickly become the hottest reservation on the island. Inspired by the French bistronomy movement, the dishes blend Taiwanese ingredients with modern international influences in a laid-back vibe. Expect beautifully presented plates full of colours and flavours, such as crunchy chicken masala skins topped with cauliflower, couscous and Indian spices, or a dainty tomato salad with king fish sashimi, shiso sorbet and rosé champagne vinaigrette. RAW specialises in biodynamic French wine, plus hand-brewed coffee from local roasters.

JAPAN

Tokyo
Architect house hall JIA,
2-3-18 Jingumae, Shibuya Ku, Tokyo

**CHEF'S
COUNTER**

◆ TO VISIT BEFORE YOU DIE BECAUSE
You would try the 'Dentucky Fried Chicken' and keep the carton, customised with your own pictures.

In the heart of Jingumae district in Tokyo, chef Zaiyu Hasegawa pushes the potential of Japanese dining well beyond the boundaries of centuries-old Japanese traditions, creating an innovative cuisine served with humour and fun. The chef's intention is to bring people together over good food via a casual dining experience, communicating with the guests through the open kitchen. The omakase tasting menu incorporates influences from around the world, and expresses the chef's sense of humour. Highlights include his now-trademark reinterpretation of fast-food chicken wings named 'Dentucky Fried Chicken', and a superlative 20-ingredient salad, mostly sourced from the garden of the chef's sister. The front-of-house team, led by Hasegawa's wife, embraces the traditional Japanese philosophy of welcoming every diner with warmth and making them feel part of the Den family.

— 135 —
FLORILÈGE

JAPAN

Tokyo
B1 Seizan Gaien, 2-5-4, Jingumae,
Shibuya ward, Tokyo

MODERN FRENCH-JAPANESE

◆ TO VISIT BEFORE YOU DIE BECAUSE

The Monet's lilypads cocktail made with flowers, and inspired by
the Impressionist painter is innovative.

Florilège, meaning anthology in French, is located in Shibuya in Tokyo. Chef Hiroyasu Kawate made the decision to specialise in French food at high school and spent his formative kitchen years in Paris. He has also worked in some of Tokyo's most famous restaurants, including Quintessence. In the dining room, a bar frames the open kitchen, which is spotlit like a stage. Here the chef cooks his imaginative cuisine, combining the exquisite styles and techniques of French cuisine with the freshest Japanese produce. Through a philosophy of sustainability and a consciousness of reducing food waste, Kawate also aims to support local farmers and producers who are producing superior-quality products. The restaurant's signature dishes include hazelnut meringue and foie gras, manjū dumplings stuffed with pigeon and simmered in wine, and a sustainable beef carpaccio made with meat from Miyazaki cows.

www.aoyama-florilege.jp

— 136 —
NARISAWA

JAPAN

Tokyo
Minami Aoyama 2-6-15, Minato-ku, Tokyo

MODERN
JAPANESE

Here you can try koji, the fermented rice used to make sake, which the chef serves in an ice cream with a camellia leaf.

At its most refined, Japanese cooking is directly connected to the seasons. It is this philosophy that drives chef Yoshihiro Narisawa, whose style reflects the balance of nature and a respect for the environment. He has worked in some of Europe's most venerated kitchens, including those of Joël Robuchon and Paul Bocuse, and is deeply connected to his environment, visiting all the producers and liaising directly with them. Narisawa calls this cuisine 'innovative satoyama': sato is a place where people live, like a village or community, and yama means mountain. Together, they reference a limited space between the sea and forests, where people and nature coexist. The menu comprises sustainable ingredients like java beans and tomatoes on a hamaguri clam, his signature soil soup of burdock root fried with earth, and roasted Hida Wagyu beef rump rolled in carbonised leek 'powder', making the outside of the beef appear like charcoal.

www.narisawa-yoshihiro.com

— 137 —
SUSHI SAITO

JAPAN

Tokyo
1st Floor, Ark Hills South Tower, 1-4-5 Roppongi, Minato-ku, Tokyo

JAPANESE OMAKASE

◆ TO VISIT BEFORE YOU DIE BECAUSE

Here you can experience 'the best sushi restaurant in the world' according to the late chef Joël Robuchon.

Described by the late chef Joël Robuchon as the 'best sushi restaurant in the world', the tiny eight-person dining room is one of Japan's most venerated sushi restaurants. Chef-patron Takashi Saito is among the youngest and most outgoing sushi chefs in the country, which gives a more relaxed atmosphere to the experience than many other Michelin-starred restaurants. In a procession of precisely prepared sushi from aji (horse mackerel) with grated ginger and negi (scallions) to different cuts of tuna, Saito serves slightly smaller slices of fish than most and adds a little salt to his mild red vinegar rice. Securing a reservation is a challenge. The best bet is to try to get an invite from a regular or hire the private dining room, which has its own counter.

web.facebook.com/pages/Sushi-Saito

TAKAZAWA

JAPAN	Tokyo 3 Chome-5-2 Akasaka, Tokyo 107-0052	MODERN FRENCH-JAPANESE

◆ TO VISIT BEFORE YOU DIE BECAUSE

Each guest will receive the close personal attention of the chef and his wife, Akiko, in a futurist setting.

Once known as Aronia de Takazawa, named after the superfruit aronia as a metaphor for a little-known source of great potential, this restaurant now simply takes the moniker of the Japanese chef Yoshiaki Takazawa. Here he creates a series of contemporary and playful Japanese dishes served in visually intriguing presentations in an exclusive ten-table futurist decor. At the centre of the dining room, the experience feels intimate and exclusive when the chef prepares complex French-Japanese fusion dishes alone in the open kitchen. The signature 'ratatouille' is a mosaic-like terrine of different-coloured vegetables, which have been prepared in various ways, while 'salt' features a lightly battered ayu fish served with colourful dots of flavoured salts.

— 139 —
MICHEL BRAS TOYA

JAPAN

Toyako-cho
Shimizu, Toyako-cho, Abuta-gun,
Hokkaido, 049-5722

**MODERN
FRENCH**

◆ TO VISIT BEFORE YOU DIE BECAUSE

The bay window offers one of the most stunning views of Lake Toya.

Stunned by the natural landscape of Lake Toya and its surroundings in Hokkaido, chef Michel Bras and his son Sébastien decided it would be a perfect location to establish their cuisine, with a breathtaking view of the region. They visited local farmers to develop the best of the terroir in the brilliant colours, aromas, tastes, flowing movement and sensory elegance of the famed specialty 'gargouillou', the chef's signature dish. Another specialty is 'coulant', a dessert whose contrasts of temperature and texture, and the chocolate flavour become one on the plate. It has been copied throughout the world and is said to evoke supreme bliss.

www.windsor-hotels.co.jp

— 140 —
LOCAVORE

INDONESIA (BALI)

Ubud
10 Jalan Dewi Sita, Ubud, Bali

MODERN INDONESIAN

◆ TO VISIT BEFORE YOU DIE BECAUSE

You would taste the cocktails in their hidden Night Rooster bar, just across the street from the restaurant, which features ten drinks based on seasonal local fruits and vegetables.

At Locavore, in mountainous Ubud, the cuisine is based on hyper-local ingredients, celebrating the farmers, fishers and food artisans of Indonesia while using modern European cooking techniques. The culinary duo, Dutch-born Eelke Plasmeijer and Indonesian Ray Adriansyah, have a nose-to-tail philosophy, and share the origin of all their ingredients on the menu. Both their Locavore and Herbivore tasting menus feature a wide variety of dishes prepared with local ingredients, such as raw Balinese abalone, Sumbawa Island oysters, and beef short ribs from Java. Even the plates, silverware and cocktail glasses are made in nearby workshops.

— 141 —
BHAIRO, TAJ LAKE PALACE

INDIA

Udaipur
Taj Lake Palace, Udaipur, Rajasthan 313001

TRADITIONAL INDIAN

◆ TO VISIT BEFORE YOU DIE BECAUSE

You would dine on the Mewar Terrace, in an intimate domed pavilion for two, overlooking one of the most beautiful lakes on earth.

With its marble palaces and five lakes encircled by hills, Udaipur is one of India's most spellbinding places. Framed by the backdrop of the striking Aravalli Hills, the luxurious Taj Lake Palace was built in 1746 by Maharana Jagat Singh II, the 62nd successor to the royal dynasty of Mewar. The unique and opulent marble setting is accessible only by boat, and encompasses four acres of graceful courtyards, pavilions and gardens with a refreshing lakeside swimming pool. At Bhairo rooftop restaurant, the moonlit view and ambience are unique. Widely spaced, linen-dressed tables with wicker armchairs hug the edge of the deck. As birds wing slowly by, and the shoreline begins to twinkle with lights, the atmosphere of this contemporary European-Asian restaurant will enchant you.

www.taj.tajhotels.com

— 142 —
WADI RUM NIGHT LUXURY CAMP

Wadi Rum

JORDAN

Anfeshiah, Wadi Rum Protected Area and
Natural Reserve, Wadi Rum 00962

TRADITIONAL
BEDOUIN

◆ TO VISIT BEFORE YOU DIE BECAUSE

It is a wonderful experience to smell the scents of the traditional
Bedouin barbecue coming out of the ground while you are watching
the stars in perfect silence.

Located in the desert valley of Wadi Rum, one of the most beautiful deserts in the world, Wadi Rum Night Luxury Camp is decorated in a Bedouin style with spacious tents furnished with kingsize beds clad in smart linens, wrought-iron lanterns and hand-carved wooden furniture. At night, meals take place in a large communal Bedouin tent, upholstered in Jordanian textiles, where seating can be on the carpeted floor or higher up on cushions, and creamy hummus and labneh sprinkled with olive oil and za'atar, marinated olives and plates of crunchy fresh fatoush salad are all served with just-baked shrak flatbread. The real treat of the experience is zarb, the traditional Bedouin barbecue that is more like a ceremony than a meal, with a slow-roast in a charcoal-filled pit dug deep into the desert sand.

www.wadirumnight.com

OMAN	**Zighy Bay** Zighy Bay, Musandam Peninsula Sultanate of Oman, 800 Dibba	**TRADITIONAL MIDDLE EAST**

◆ TO VISIT BEFORE YOU DIE BECAUSE

Here you can take a cooking class in Spice Market, the resort's Arabic restaurant, and learn an easy local recipe to make at home.

Six Senses Zighy Bay is a hidden gem, located on Oman's northern Musandam Peninsula; it is only a two-hour car journey from Dubai, but a world apart. The resort is as spectacular as its setting, with mountains on one side and a long sandy beach on the other. Perched on a clifftop 293 metres above sea level, its contemporary signature restaurant, Sense on the Edge, is the perfect place to enjoy a very memorable evening, with views overlooking the bay. With the lights from the resort and the adjacent Zighy Village glittering below like fireflies, diners will enjoy the most romantic evening, eating traditional dishes created from the vegetables grown in the resort's organic garden.

— 144 —
ORANA

AUSTRALIA

Adelaide
1/285 Rundle Street,
Adelaide SA 5000

**MODERN
AUSTRALIAN**

◆ TO VISIT BEFORE YOU DIE BECAUSE

You will discover the beautiful stories chef Jack Zonfrillo has learnt from the local Aboriginal communities through the way he has created his menu.

Chef Jock Zonfrillo was born in Scotland, with Italian roots. In his tentable restaurant, Orana, which means 'welcome' in some aboriginal languages, he is dedicated to expressing his love for Australia's unique ingredients and aboriginal food culture. He buys the 65 native ingredients on the menu directly from these local communities to ensure money goes straight to the source, working with the seasons and constantly changing the menu accordingly. Using all Australian proteins – kangaroo, scallops, marron, buffalo and emu – Zonfrillo adds to his refined creations fruits like riberries and native cherries, and local herbs such as aniseed myrtle and mountain pepper. Depending on the time of year, diners will learn more about karbala (a beach succulent) or gibing (a native plum), and taste extraordinary dishes.

restaurantorana.com

IGNI

AUSTRALIA	Geelong	MODERN AUSTRALIAN
	Ryan Place, Geelong, Victoria 3220	

◆ TO VISIT BEFORE YOU DIE BECAUSE

Chef Aaron Turner's brilliant dish of potatoes, sliced into thin noodles, cooked in potato-starch water, tossed in garlic butter and spiked with the purple flowers is a must-try.

Igni (Latin for 'from fire') offers a beautifully crafted and worthwhile experience. In a location that might be difficult to find, the whole journey starts with the buzz from just tracking it down to one of the back streets of Geelong. In an intimate yet sophisticated space with polished concrete floors and charcoal grey curtains, the young chef Aaron Turner, who trained at Noma (Copenhagen) and El Celler de Can Roca (Girona), cooks over the ashes of his charcoal-grill with the best seasonal and regional ingredients. Do not expect a menu: the only choice diners have to make is either five or eight courses. The creations are then tailored for each table, after a conversation with the staff regarding the products available each day. Turner's fire-fuelled cooking is sharp and confident and his creations brilliant. The meal begins with small snacks, from grilled baby zucchini flowers with slightly grilled local mussels, to saltbush leaves that are dusted with vinegar powder. To follow, there will be raw calamari sliced into thin ribbons tossed with tiny salty-sweet berries moisturised by chicken broth, or lightly grilled marron teamed with fermented pickled cucumbers and a butter sauce flavoured with fish stock and sherry vinegar.

— 146 —
ATTICA

AUSTRALIA

Melbourne
74 Glen Eira Road, Ripponlea, Victoria 3185

MODERN AUSTRALIAN

◆ TO VISIT BEFORE YOU DIE BECAUSE

After dinner, chef Ben Shewry will welcome you in the garden to discuss herbs over a cup of tea and snacks.

In a former bank in the Ripponlea neighbourhood of Melbourne, Attica has an atmosphere that is dark and modern, with white linen on the tables and elegant pools of light. Ben Shewry is the chef who redefined Australian cuisine. Raised in New Zealand on a remote farm and educated in a school of just seven pupils, he grew up collecting bays and abalones barefoot. Determined to be a chef since he was five, Shewry worked in his first kitchen at the age of ten and has apprenticed under talented chefs such as Andrew McConnell (Cutler & Co., Melbourne) and David Thompson (Nahm, Bangkok). Passionate about

Australian native cuisine, Shewry offers a unique and personal menu inspired by taste memories from his childhood, using bush ingredients like quandong, paperbark, pearl meat and lemon myrtle. Diners could also taste a salted raw red kangaroo with native bunya nuts and purple carrots, and fresh abalone in its shell, paired with a delicate glass of sake mixed with Riesling wine. Two of his most famous creations were prompted by near-death experiences: being dragged out to sea while collecting mussels ('Sea Tastes') and outrunning a volcanic eruption at Mount Ruapehu on his snowboard ('Snow Crab').

www.attica.com.au

AUSTRALIA

Melbourne
17 Market Ln, Melbourne VIC 3000

**TRADITIONAL
CANTONESE**

◆ TO VISIT BEFORE YOU DIE BECAUSE

Here you will experience the most refined traditional Cantonese restaurant outside of China, among the best in the world.

In a red-carpeted dining room with classical Chinese lacquered wood details, Flower Drum has had a fearsome reputation for over 35 years in Melbourne, with regulars greeted by name. Named after a Rodgers and Hammerstein musical about expatriated Chinese people and their lives in America, Flower Drum's Cantonese and Sichuan menu is rooted in tradition and changes with the seasons. At the tables, waiters who have been there for more than 20 years serve refined Xiao long bao (juicy dumplings), shaped in perfect pouches of fresh crab suspended in a rich seafood liquor, and the Peking duck is served on a traditional wheeled trolley, bearing spring onions, plum sauce and crisp-skinned meat with warm pancakes.

— 148 —
BENNELONG

AUSTRALIA

Sydney
Sydney Opera House, Bennelong Point,
Sydney, NSW 2000

**MODERN
AUSTRALIAN**

◆ TO VISIT BEFORE YOU DIE BECAUSE

**It is an amazing experience to taste the meringue-based dessert, tribute to
Bennelong's incredible architecture, in front of the harbour bridge.**

Since its opening, Bennelong has become a landmark in Sydney. People gather here to drink cocktails at the upper bar, share a fine-dining menu at the restaurant downstairs, or sit at the Cured and Cultured bar counter right in the middle of the action, to sip fresh champagne with South Coast oysters. Peter Gilmore is the executive chef of Bennelong and its sister restaurant Quay, both situated at the edge of Sydney Harbour. He is a well-known figure in Australia's vibrant food scene and serves a robust menu crafted in partnership with farmers, fishermen, breeders and providers from across the land.

www.bennelong.com.au

— 149 —
MOMOFUKU SEIOBO

AUSTRALIA

Sydney
80 Pyrmont Street, Level G, Sydney, NSW 2009

MODERN CARIBBEAN

◆ TO VISIT BEFORE YOU DIE BECAUSE

Here you can experience fun interludes in the meal, when you are given a pestle and asked to grind the mixture of plantains, garlic and chicharrones into a thick paste yourself.

Located inside Sydney's Star casino, Momofuku Seiobo was the first of David Chang's Momofuku venues to open outside New York. The exterior of the restaurant blends into its surroundings, but once inside guests are welcomed by sleek, dark interiors, creating an intimate setting. In the laid-back atmosphere with loud music, the luckiest diners will be seated at the counter to enjoy a behind-the-scenes show as each of their dishes is prepared and plated in front of them. Chef Paul Carmichael, originally from Barbados, serves a unique 14-course tasting menu inspired by his exotic roots: the fried chicken sandwich is filled with a thrillingly spicy sauce, and the Caribbean cou-cou dish (the national dish of Barbados) is dressed up with caviar.

— 150 —
BRAE

AUSTRALIA

Victoria
4285 Cape Otway Road,
Birregurra, Victoria 3242

**FARM-TO-TABLE/
MODERN
AUSTRALIAN**

◆ TO VISIT BEFORE YOU DIE BECAUSE

It is a real treat to wake up in one of the six luxury eco-friendly guest suites to the smell of wood-fired sourdough bread served for breakfast with homemade jams.

Chef Dan Hunter's cooking career has taken him around the globe and into the kitchens of some of the world's most acclaimed restaurants, such as Mugaritz in Spain. Returning to Australia, he led the kitchen of Dunkeld's Royal Mail Hotel where he developed his first intensive organic kitchen garden programme, before starting his first solo venture at Brae. Set in Victoria's Otway hinterland among 30 acres of vegetable plots and orchards, the old farm has been transformed by Hunter into a beautiful countryside house filled with Australian art, while maintaining the wood-fired oven and farm-to-table ethos. Hunter grows organic fruits and vegetables and uses only ethically grown produce from the surrounding area and local farmers, to offer a contemporary cuisine based on respect for nature and seasonality. The 16-course menu starts with colourful crunchy snacks like edible flowers and oyster ice cream in its shell and leads to Wagyu short ribs with Otway shiitake mushrooms and finger lime cells.

braerestaurant.com

About the author

Amélie Vincent is a digital influencer, food writer, artistic director and photographer specialized in the international food scene. She is the first official TasteHunter of the World's 50 Best Restaurants, hunting for new culinary talents, and organizing culinary events, all around the world.
Her agency The Foodalist is specialized in gastronomy PR and contents production for various magazines, tv channels, chefs, and brands (@thefoodalist, www.thefoodalist.com).

Amélie is also a tv host and writes books reflecting about the international food scene. She was born in Brussels, though in the meantime has studied and worked as an Intellectual Property lawyer on 3 different continents before ultimately moving back to Europe. Today, Amélie divides her time between Paris and Brussels, though she might be known to make a quick stop in London and Hong Kong within the same week.

with chef Hiroyasu Kawate

with chef Bo Bech

with chef Alex Atala

with chef Vladimir Mukhin

with chef Gaggan Anand

with chef Sergio Herman

with chef Joan Roca

with chefs Gastón Acurio and Alain Ducasse

with chefs Gaggan Anand and Mauro Colagreco

with chefs Alain Ducasse and David Lai

with chef Riccardo Camanini

with chef Massimo Bottura

with chef Paul Pairet

with chef Alain Ducasse

with chefs Yoshihiro Narisawa and Mauro Colagreco

with chef Josean Alija

with chef Richard Ekkebus

with chef Sang-Hoon Degeimbre

with chefs Gert De Mangeleer and Zaiyu Hasegawa

with chef Dominique Crenn

with chef Diego Rossi

with chefs Yannick Alleno and Alain Passard

Index

Photo credits

p. 9 Merry de Dreux-Brézé, p. 10-11 Tasting Counter, p. 12-15 Aman, p. 16-17 Anthony Tahlier, p. 18 Galdones Photography, p. 19 Niels Famaey, p. 20 Astrid y Gaston/Pocho Caceres, p. 21 César del Rio, p. 22 Amélie Vincent - The Foodalist, p. 23 Anne Fishbein, p. 24 Charity Burggraaf, p. 25-27 Mil, p. 28-29 Pujol, p. 30-31 Quintonil, p. 32 Sud 777, p. 33 Lorea, p. 34 The Catbird Seat, p. 35 The Neighbourhood Dining Group, photo Andrea Behrends, p. 36-37 Ingrid Hofstra, p. 38 Matty Yangwoo Kim, p. 39 Jake Chessum, p. 40 Amélie Vincent - The Foodalist, p. 41 Blackletter, p. 42-43 Zack DeZon, p. 44-45 Corry Arnold, p. 46-47 Evan Sung, p. 48 Amélie Vincent - The Foodalist, p. 49 Courtesy of Estela, photo Tuukka Koski, p. 50-51 Amélie Vincent - The Foodalist, p. 52-53 Lynn Donaldson, p. 54-57 Eric Wolfinger, p. 58 Anders Husa, p. 59 Claudio Vera, p. 60 DOM, photo Ricardo D'Angelo, p. 61 DOM, photo Rubens Kato, p. 62-63 Anders Husa, p. 64 Amélie Vincent - The Foodalist, p. 65 Stefania Spadoni, p. 66-67 Mitchell van Voorbergen, p. 68-71 Pieter D'Hoop for The Jane Antwerp, p. 72-73 Amélie Vincent - The Foodalist, p. 74-75 Anders Husa, p. 76-79 Adrià Goula, p. 80-81 Pepo Segura, p. 82 Amélie Vincent - The Foodalist, p. 83 Pedro Cortacans, p. 84-85 Staffan Sundström, p. 86-87 Andoni Epelde, p. 88-89 Jose Luis Lopez de Zubiria, p. 90-91 Amélie Vincent - The Foodalist, p. 92-93 Claes Bech-Poulsen, p. 94-97 Amélie Vincent - The Foodalist, p. 98 Amélie Vincent - The Foodalist, p. 99 Jason Loucas, p. 100-101 José Luis López de Zubiría/Mugaritz, p. 102-105 Amélie Vincent - The Foodalist, p. 106 Piet Dekersgieter, p. 107 Amélie Vincent - The Foodalist, p. 108 Amélie Vincent - The Foodalist, p. 109 El Celler de Can Roca, p. 110 Per Nagel, p. 111 Amélie Vincent - The Foodalist, p. 112 Mikla, p. 113 Amélie Vincent - The Foodalist, p. 114-115 Soho House Istanbul, p. 116-117 Anders Husa, p. 118 Amélie Vincent - The Foodalist, p. 119-121 Amélie Vincent - The Foodalist, p. 122-125 Claes Bech-Poulsen, p. 126-130 Amélie Vincent - The Foodalist, p. 131 Bubble Dogs Kitchen Table, p. 132 Emma Lee Photography, p. 133 Peden and Munk, p. 134-135 João Wengorovius, p. 136 Jake Eastham, p. 137 Per-Anders Jorgensen, p. 138-141 Ed Reeve, p. 142-143 courtesy of the Blue Mountain School, p. 144-145 Amélie Vincent - The Foodalist, p. 146 Diverxo, p. 147 Daniel Berlin Restaurant, p. 148-149 Amélie Vincent - The Foodalist, p. 150 Eduardo Torres, p. 151-153 Amélie Vincent - The Foodalist, p. 154 Callo Albanese & Sueo, p. 155-159 Amélie Vincent - The Foodalist, p. 160-161 Jean-Christophe Leroux, p. 162-163 Maaemo, p. 164 Elodie Ganger, p. 165 Marie-Pierre Morel, p. 166-169 Amélie Vincent - The Foodalist, p. 170-173 Pierre Monetta, p. 174-175 Hirama, p. 176-177 Amélie Vincent - The Foodalist, p. 178 Sergio Coimbra, p. 179-181 Amélie Vincent - The Foodalist, p. 182 Johan Strindberg, p. 183 Helén Pe, p. 184-187 Martin Botvidsson/Stefan Gissberg, p. 188-189 Amélie Vincent - The Foodalist, p. 190 Image Select, p. 191 Amélie Vincent - The Foodalist, p. 192-193 Marie-Pierre Morel, p. 194 Amélie Vincent - The Foodalist, p. 195 De Librije, p. 196-197 Justin Patrick, p. 198 Amélie Vincent - The Foodalist, p. 199 COMO Metropolitan Bangkok, p. 200-201 Paste, p. 202-203 Amélie Vincent - The Foodalist, p. 204-205 Tanya Traboulsi, p. 206-207 Amélie Vincent - The Foodalist, p. 208-209 Amélie Vincent - The Foodalist, p. 210-211 Amélie Vincent - The Foodalist, p. 212 Antonina Gern, p. 213 Shashank Das, p. 214-215 Aman, p. 216 Jungheelee, p. 217 Mingles, p. 218 Scott Wright of Limelight Studio, p. 219-221 Amélie Vincent - The Foodalist, p. 222-223 Odette Restaurant, p. 224 Shinichiro Fujii, p. 225 RAW Taipei, p. 226-227 Shinichiro Fujii & JESTO, p. 228 Florilège, p. 229 Narisawa, p. 230 Aiste Miseviciute, p. 231 Yuji Honda, p. 232 Windsor Hotel Toya, p. 233 Locavore, p. 234-237 Bhairo, Taj Lake Palace, p. 238 Image Select, p. 239 John Athimaritis, p. 240 Restaurant Orana, p. 241-243 Amélie Vincent - The Foodalist, p. 244 right Amélie Vincent - The Foodalist, left Colin Page, p. 245 Amélie Vincent - The Foodalist, p. 246 Image Select, p. 247 Nick Scott, p. 248-253 Amélie Vincent - The Foodalist

Colophon

All Texts
Amélie Vincent – The Foodalist

Copy-editing
Linda Schofield
Robert Fulton

all images (except see p. 255):
Amélie Vincent – The Foodalist

Back Cover Image:
Interior of Sketch, London

Book Design
ASB

This book is
MARKED

MARKED is an initiative
by Lannoo Publishers
www.marked-books.com

Sign up for our MARKED newsletter with news
about new and forthcoming publications on art,
interior design, food & travel, photography and
fashion as well as exclusive offers and events.

If you have any questions or comments about
the material in this book, please do not hesitate
to contact our editorial team: markedteam@
lannoo.com

© Lannoo publishers, Belgium, 2019
D/2019/45/198 – NUR 440
ISBN: 978 94 014 5442 1

www.lannoo.com

#AREYOUMARKED